The art of
ALIVENESS

The art of ALIVENESS

A CREATIVE RETURN TO WHAT MATTERS MOST

Flora Bowley

Hierophantpublishing

Cover design by Laura Beers
Cover art by Flora Bowley
Cover photo by Zippy Lomax
Print book interior design by Frame25 Productions

Hierophant Publishing
8301 Broadway, Suite 219
San Antonio, TX 78209
www.hierophantpublishing.com

If you are unable to order this book from your local bookseller,
you may order directly from the publisher.

Library of Congress Control Number: 2020951267

ISBN: 978-1-950253-10-4

10 9 8 7 6 5 4 3 2

To my grandparents, Max and Arlene,
for coloring outside the lines.

Contents

Foreword

In March 2016, my fiancé John died in my arms.

It was one of the most horrifying and gorgeous experiences of my life.

I didn't truly recognize the gorgeousness until some years later, when I realized that in the moment of his physical departure and in all the time since, I felt and feel such incredible love as a result of having known and loved him.

I am still learning so much about creating love and letting love be created through me. John's love for me opened my heart completely and allowed a new love partner to find me.

Perhaps you have also experienced horrifying loss or grief in your life. Most of us know this kind of horror in some form. Maybe an experience like this has never felt gorgeous to you.

In my experience, horrifying and gorgeous go together—that's how it works for me. That's my way of being present and alchemizing the wonderfull and terrible things—from the light to dark and all the places in between.

I believe that when we can welcome life and all it offers us, we can choose to meet it with our full selves and hearts and invite a transformation to take place inside of us.

This is the best way I know to be the most alive, most full, and most love-activated human being I can be. There's a kind of art to living in this way, and death—as it turns out—is also an experience of aliveness.

Flora Bowley calls this the Art of Aliveness.

This book is a kind of treasure map. The treasure itself is a beautifull precious mystery: aliveness itself.

Painting, writing, living, loving . . . there's an art to all of it, and it all takes considerable practice.

You have to keep doing it, again and again, experimenting to find out what works and what doesn't—and then keep going. This book is full of ways to practice the art of aliveness, ways to feel your own aliveness with your own inner treasure map.

And just as in any good treasure hunt, there will be obstacles.

There's the gigantic sea monster representing your inner critics—spewing out frothy proclamations of fear and regret. There's a siren song that numbs your senses and puts you to sleep while your little lifeboat drifts off course. And there are the very rocky shores of low self-esteem and overwhelm, and the thick under-growths of conformity and anxiety.

But in the midst of all of this, you have a magnificent superpower.

It's called creativity.

This is the fuel for your exploration of aliveness and for all the times you don't feel like exploring at all.

Creativity and its partner imagination flow brightly through these pages. This book is full of inspiration to bring your own kind of magic to each moment— to inspire your own curiosity and desire for play and make more alive choices.

The obstacles won't go away, and that's okay. After all, surviving obstacles brings you an awareness and strength you wouldn't know otherwise. In your practice of aliveness, you begin to notice the voices of your inner critics when they arise sooner, and you learn to meet them with love and patience. You accept and learn to understand the ebbs and flows of your energies and allow the beauty and the pain that live side by side in each moment.

Throughout it all, each of us has this creative superpower—and every one of us has the magnificent opportunity to be an artist of life.

In my own life, I use and have used the power of creativity to transform the obstacles in my life. I'm a survivor of childhood incest, I've lived in poverty, and I've suffered with anxiety and addictions. I've blocked my own creative gifts and hidden from sharing them for many years.

None of these past experiences describe or define my current life, and the catalyst for the transformations I have experienced has always been a willingness to go within, embrace all that I find, and respond creatively with my full heart. I live and practice my aliveness in the marvelous messy middle, with all the successes and challenges and everything in between.

I believe that experimenting in these ways has allowed me to transform almost any situation or feeling, no matter what changes or losses have occurred— and I'm all-ways practicing.

We live in terrifying and magical times, and we can sometimes feel depleted, assaulted, or underwater. Yet we yearn for connection, for magic, for imagination in action. How can we even begin to feel truly alive in times like these? Is it possible? What's missing from our lives? What have we forgotten?

I believe that we must reignite the power of our creative spark.

What sparks you is what wakes you.

What wakes you is what replenishes your energy.

And this process is what brings you alive.

I met Flora in person the same year that John died. I had admired her work for years and had contacted her to see whether we might want to create something together.

In our first meeting, she told me that twenty-five years earlier, my work as an artist and author had inspired her to step more confidently onto her own creative path. As I read her luscious book today and create this foreword for it, I am so glad to say that the inspiration has come full circle. We creatively spark each other.

What about you? What creatively sparks you? What dreams and desires have you hidden away from view? What tugs at your soul, aching to be expressed in the world?

What haven't you yet asked for?

Once you discover and connect with your own creative spark, you can use it to transform your life. Your curiosity will lead to new discoveries to share with the world, whether through art or words you create or just in the simple you-ness of you living life.

It's time.

It already happened that you connected with this book. Now all you need to do is accept the invitation in these pages to discover your own aliveness and put it into more practice.

This is the way forward in a world that sometimes feels broken, according to mystic and theologian Howard Thurman. "Don't ask what the world needs," he says. "Ask what makes you come alive, and go do it. Because what the world needs is people who have come alive."

This book and treasuring map will support and inspire you to come alive in new ways and let the world experience those great gifts in your soul.

Love,

SARK (Susan Ariel Rainbow Kennedy)

Introduction

*It is a serious thing just to be alive on
this fresh morning in the broken world.*
—Mary Oliver

When my first painting professor walked into the room and said, "Well, we all have a thousand bad paintings in us, so let's get going," I caught my breath.

That was a lot of bad paintings.

As a nineteen-year-old art student sitting in my first college art class, I loved how this place made me feel. The rich smell of turpentine, the worn wooden easels, the it's-OK-to-make-a-mess paint-splattered everything—it all made me feel alive. Like anything was possible.

Looking back, I realize those daunting and discouraging words struck a lasting chord. I would spend the next two decades of my life painting at least a thousand good and bad paintings, and in the process I would come to understand that the simple act of applying paint to canvas had become my life's greatest teacher.

Fast-forward over twenty-five years, and I can say with heartfelt certainty and deep gratitude that the creative process has informed and seeped into every aspect of how I live my life.

Like a dear friend, painting has guided me through the deepest valleys of loss and lifted me to the highest peaks of joy and release. It has gently taken my hands and shown me why letting go creates space for more magic and how change is not only necessary but life-giving. Painting has given me a safe space to get lost and find myself again inside the great unknown, and it has reminded me time and time again that following my heart will always lead me home.

Ultimately, what I've learned from painting is that artmaking is a practice, and the practice of making art is also a practice in living.

I've always thought of artists as changemakers and paradigm shifters. Hungry for inspiration, they dip below the visible surface of the everyday, alchemize what they experience there, and create innovative portals into new ways of doing and being. Having the opportunity to be an artist in this lifetime and to view the world through the lens of a maker has always felt like a profound honor and privilege. What I've come to understand through my own experience is that the very same tools and principles that artists cultivate can also be applied to life.

Whether we're creating a painting or creating a life, our willingness to step into mystery, cultivate connection to what matters most, and let go of what is no longer serving us will always move our story forward.

I imagine I will always love pushing colors around a canvas, but over the years, the dynamic parallels I've discovered between art and life have become even more fascinating to me than the act of painting alone ever was. This lifelong exploration is what this book is all about.

It is my deepest hope that the intimate perspectives I've gained through decades of dancing with my own creative muse may serve to spark a beautiful reunion between you and your own aliveness—no paints required.

The Art of Aliveness is about the potent place where the lessons we glean through creative practices offer meaning, direction, and depth to our everyday life experiences. In return, the lessons we learn in life also inform our creative work. In the end, creativity becomes a way of life, and a creative current infuses life so thoroughly that there's really no distinction between the two.

When I talk about *aliveness* in this context, it goes well beyond sleeping, eating, breathing, and going through the motions of responsibilities. Aliveness means reaching into the vast depths of our full human experience, not shying away from what we find there, and being brave enough to say, "I can be with what is, and I can choose again. I can create beauty out of sorrow and find meaning in the madness. I can be the alchemist of my own life no matter what cards I've been dealt."

My own pursuit of aliveness has led me to ask the following questions, which are at the core of this book:

* How can my life become a thoughtful and poignant work of art?

* How can my works of art be fueled by my soul's deepest longings for truth and beauty?

* How can my life and my creative offerings become seamlessly connected to one another?

Through curiosity, practice, and patience I have learned that when I take my time and honestly work both ends of this spectrum, the lines between life and art begin to blur. In the overlap between the two, the simple, profound, and complex experience of being fully alive resides. To be clear, *The Art of Aliveness* is not about being our best self, but rather becoming a more honest, inquisitive, and ever-evolving version of ourself—a work in progress and a stunning masterpiece all at the same time.

Not a day goes by that I don't reflect in some way on how painting teaches me how to live and how living teaches me how to paint. The thousands of hours I've spent at my own easel, along with the many years I've spent supporting others on their creative paths, reinforce just how powerful and transformational the creative process can be.

In each chapter of this book, I share the most compelling and useful teachings I've gained through my years as a professional painter, workshop facilitator, and creative catalyst. You'll find my own life experiences woven throughout, which have taught me about change, courage, adaptability, and truth-telling, along with gems of wisdom from students, mentors, and friends.

I hope the stories and philosophies I share here serve as keys to the doors you're ready to open. When you walk through these doors, I hope freedom, connection, and a genuine feeling of aliveness await you on the other side. This is what you deserve, and this is what I want for you.

To support you on this journey, I've included some sections called Try This On. In my painting retreats, I often encourage folks to try on whatever colors, images, or brave moves feel intriguing to them in any given moment, while remembering they can always change their minds. I believe this idea of trying something on without an attachment to the outcome ignites action, curiosity, and levity without the pressure of perfection.

With that in mind, I wholeheartedly encourage you to try on the action steps for each lesson if you choose. Nothing is required, of course, but if you want to experience the art of aliveness from the inside out, these invitations will support you in doing just that. I also suggest having a writing journal to accompany you on this exploration. I will offer questions and prompts to consider throughout the book, and giving yourself the space to write, sketch, and brainstorm on paper will serve to deepen and clarify your reflections.

We live in a rapidly changing world with many challenges, and we are all responding to the call to inhabit this earth, our communities, and our personal lives in new and inventive ways. The learning curve is steep, and many of us feel intense pressure to help find new solutions to the myriad social, political, health, and environmental problems we face. Old structures are falling apart, giving way to fresh opportunities and new ways of being. A great rearranging is underway. Now, more than ever, applying the philosophies of the creative process to our lives and to our world is not only helpful, it's vital.

I believe each and every one of us exists here for a profound purpose at this exact time. Each of us has something to contribute to the collective healing that we so desperately need. If you're holding this book right now, I believe you're ready to move through whatever fears are holding you back from experiencing your soul's deepest desires and offerings. I also believe that by connecting more intimately with what sparks your imagination and ignites your unique sense of purpose, you are taking foundational steps toward more equity, peace, and justice for all beings.

We are in this together. Let's lift each other up and remember what it feels like to be truly alive. I believe our collective timing is perfect, and it is my sincere desire that this book supports you on your brave journey home to what matters most.

This is the art of aliveness.

Start by Remembering

You've always had the power.
—Glinda the Good Witch, *The Wizard of Oz*

I practiced for weeks gearing up for my first attempt at singing a solo in my seventh-grade choir. Even so, it took everything I had just to walk up to the front of the room and stand next to the piano. With shaky hands and sweat dripping down my sides, it's no surprise that my voice completely seized the moment I began to sing. After hearing a few squeaky off-key notes and the snickering of my choirmates, everything that happened next is a blur, which is probably for the best.

I decided in that moment that I would never sing again.

Sadly, that was the end of singing for me for the next twenty-eight years. Even singing "Happy Birthday" at parties caused my throat to tighten and my palms to sweat. What if people heard how terrible I was? *I should probably just pretend to sing and save myself and everyone else the pain of having to hear my actual voice.*

So that's what I did. I stuffed it down. I avoided it at all costs. I lip-synched. I moved to the back of the room. Eventually, I forgot that once upon a time, I *loved* to sing.

Then, on my fortieth birthday, I was traveling in Spain and my dear friend Leslie Helpert, who is an incredible singer and teacher, offered to give me a free voice lesson. My mind raced with excuses as to why this was a bad idea for everyone involved. Those feelings of shame and embarrassment from seventh grade were still hardwired into my nervous system.

But somewhere, deep down, there was a part of me that was ready to sing again. A part of me that remembered that all humans are meant to express themselves in this way, that singing is a healing part of being alive.

It was also not lost on me that I had dedicated the entire previous decade of my life to helping other people move through creative blocks and fears. Who was I to not sing just because I felt a bit terrified? What was I afraid of? What would I miss out on if I stayed in my fear?

Knowing that the best things happen when we move out of our comfort zone, I showed up at Leslie's cute sixth-floor apartment in the heart of Barcelona, nerves and all. I apologized in advance for my terrible voice and rambled on about why I wasn't a singer and how I was just trying to be gracious and receive this generous gift. Meanwhile, my inner child was dancing on the rooftops. She was getting to sing again after all these years!

What happened next took me by surprise. Leslie gently guided me through all kinds of unique and creative ways to help me open up my voice through body and breath awareness, and I actually thought I sounded OK, in moments. Most importantly, it did not feel like seventh-grade choir at all.

I ended up taking voice lessons with Leslie for the next two years. And while I'm still not one to break out into a solo around a campfire, I now sing because I love how it makes me feel, regardless of how it sounds. Singing makes me feel alive.

As a painting teacher, I often hear people say things like, "I'm not an artist. I can't even draw a stick figure! I didn't get those genes." Or folks who *do* feel creatively inclined will diminish those feelings, saying things like, "Well, I'm not very good at art. I just like to dabble. It's nothing, really."

I hear these self-fulfilling stories over and over again in my line of work, and I carry my own versions of them as well. Perhaps you too have heard yourself declaring what you are or are not capable of doing?

Wherever you land on creativity spectrum, I believe it's worthwhile to take an honest look at where those stories came from, how they might be spilling over into other parts of your life, and what they are keeping you from experiencing. So often these beliefs are based in old narratives, trauma, or conditions, and they simply aren't true. If we don't take time to clear out the cobwebs, they can be pesky and powerful blocks to creativity and aliveness.

Let me start by saying that I understand why creativity can be so hard to embrace. There's an enormous amount of vulnerability that goes along with creating something out of nothing, and beyond those precious early years when crayons are abundant and "art rules" don't exist, most of us don't live in a culture that encourages us to explore a creative path. In fact, the opposite seems to be true.

Even though I grew up surrounded by my dad's paintings, an aunt who owned an art gallery, and plenty of support to explore my own creativity, I certainly thought only a few Artists with a capital A could be "real artists." Besides these elusive and celebrated few (who were mostly men), most creatives didn't seem to be taken very seriously.

I can't tell you how many skeptical looks and raised eyebrows I've received for simply stating, "I'm an artist." More often than not, I'm met with a dismissive or disbelieving response, which speaks volumes to the lack of respect many creatives face. Factor in the widely accepted perceptions of the starving and/ or self-destructive artist, and it makes perfect sense that most people feel a need to disassociate themselves from their creative spirits. Why would anyone choose the lawless and unpredictable path of being a creative when so many other well-traveled options exist? Seems pretty risky.

Unfortunately, the old-school beliefs about who gets to be a capital A Artist (the magical chosen few) and who doesn't (everyone else) allow us to forget that creativity and being alive go hand in hand, like a brilliant birthright given to each of us with our very first breath.

And while choosing to be a professional artist is one very specific and dedicated creative journey, there's a vibrant world of opportunities to engage with creativity that live just off that beaten path. Artmaking and creative thinking serve as powerful vehicles to access more of our own humanity and create a life we truly love. The good news is that this kind of exploration is available to anyone who is courageous and curious enough to take the first step. Exploring this exhilarating terrain is what the art of aliveness is all about.

The Full Spectrum of Creativity
To remember why creativity is so essential, take a moment to imagine life without it. We would miss out on so much of what makes being alive exquisite: music, poetry, dance, literature, theater, new inventions, and so much more are inextricably linked to human creativity.

However, there are also more integrated and subtle ways that creativity shows up and elevates our day-to-day experiences—things you might do naturally without considering them to be creative acts at all.

Let's take a moment to broaden the definition of what creativity means by considering how simple acts of observation, curiosity, and innovation hold the power to bring more life to otherwise mundane moments.

Imagine walking down the street and reveling in the way light and shadows dance across the sidewalk or the way an orange leaf pops against the blue sky. What about composing a handwritten letter to someone you love? Or how about arranging the items in your home to reflect more of your personal style? Can you imagine a morning practice that includes a few minutes with an evocative writing prompt or experimenting with the way watercolors swirl and merge together on a piece of paper? Can you remember the last time you moved your body to one of your favorite songs simply for the joy it brings? How have you used creative problem-solving to come up with new solutions in your personal relationships?

Creative adventures can be as messy or involved as you choose, but they don't need to be fancy, groundbreaking, or even take a lot of time to be valid and effective. In fact, simple acts of creative expression and innovation woven into daily life have an incredible way of soothing, stirring, and reminding us what it feels like to be alive. In turn, flexing our creative muscles fortifies our ability to be more tuned in, observant, and adaptable in all parts of our life.

In this way, fortifying any strand of our creative web strengthens the whole. The principles and philosophies that drive the creative process also have the power to infuse life with the same richness that the actual act of creating so poignantly reveals.

In other words, creativity goes well beyond making stuff. It's a mindset—a way of being that is the opposite of productivity for productivity's sake. Creativity synthesizes our life experiences and inspires us to dream things into being. In this way, your unique expression, whether through song, dance, paint, verse, activism, gardening, fabric, food, or love, serves as a contribution and gift to the world around you.

Take a moment to reflect on the many ways you already infuse your daily life with creativity:

* Are you the kind of person who delights in seeing bird silhouettes against a stormy sky?

* Do you find great satisfaction in adding a little pop of color to your outfit?

* Do you seek out new and interesting ways to prepare food and perhaps learn a bit about a new culture along the way?

* Do you love stringing words together, even if they are just notes in your journal?

* Do you come up with weird and wonderful games to play at parties?

* Do you enjoy visualizing new ways the world might become a more equitable place for all beings?

* What other ways do you weave creativity into your everyday experiences, perhaps without even trying?

You're just being you—noticing, engaging, and creating as you move through life—and *that* is the art of aliveness in its purest form.

Of course, many of us have what I call "creative wounds." Like my experience in seventh-grade choir, there are times when courageous creative endeavors do not go as planned. We might experience shame or be discouraged from pursuing that avenue of creativity any further. These tender experiences can lead us to stifle our impulses in certain areas or even abandon creative pursuits altogether.

I'm here to say that we all have the power to rewrite those stories, beginning right now.

If you're reading this and feeling disconnected from your creative spirit in some way, I believe you've already begun the journey back to it. The way I see it, being fully honest about what is absent in our lives is actually one of the most profound ways to become reunited with what makes us whole again.

When we begin to engage in creative practices, we start to move the energy of life that is within us. When this energy is sparked, we can't help becoming more open, present, and connected to possibilities that exist beyond the obvious options laid out before us. Suddenly, we are in charge again. From this place of empowerment, we're reminded that we have options, we are calling the shots, and we don't have to stay stuck with how things currently are.

This is creativity in motion.

You don't need to create something that feels beautiful or useful. You don't even need to create *a thing* at all. Over time, the practice of creating teaches us to value ourselves for showing up and believing that our contribution is worthy and that this feeling of aliveness is worth the risk. This is how we learn to trust ourselves as capable creators in the world, and this is how we get back in the driver's seat of our own lives.

I've seen it time and time again in my painting retreats. A student arrives feeling disconnected from her creativity and source of inspiration. She begins the process of midwifing a blank canvas through rich layers of color and mark, dark and light, feeling and sensation. Through the dance of letting go and allowing back in, becoming unstuck, and breaking through, a spark returns to her eyes. With each brushstroke and sway of her hips, the flickering remembrance of a primal creative capacity makes its way from her hands to the working surface. As she brings a painting to life before her very eyes, she's reminded that she also has the innate ability to bring *herself* to life.

Painting provides a tangible way to meet ourselves in the space where hand, paint, and canvas collide, and I'll always love painting for this tactile experience. However, living a creative life doesn't require any art supplies at all. Creating the work of art that is *your life* is available to anyone willing to embrace the tools of aliveness, even if your hands never find their way to a paintbrush.

Consciously cultivating aliveness means choosing to be courageous, intuitive, spontaneous, and discerning. It also means embracing contrast, being willing to start over, taking one small step at a time, and allowing space for the mystery of the moment to unfold.

It means choosing life.

Try This On

If your innate creative potential, either in art or life, feels buried beneath years of old stories, stagnant patterns, or forgotten dreams, please know that you're not alone. It's never too late to remember and revitalize these parts of yourself.

To support this process of remembering, I invite you to do some dreaming with me. Without feeling limited by logistical or earthly constraints, take some time to get comfortable and dream into the most realized creative version of yourself you can possibly imagine. This is a time to dream big. Don't hold back. Don't move to the back of the room.

In this practice, anything and everything is possible. Let these prompts get you started and see where your imagination wants to wander. I encourage you to have fun with it! Remember that these sections are for trying on. You don't have to commit to anything, make it perfect, or even believe it's a good idea. Just try it on and see how it feels.

In your most wildly creative dream life, where do you live? What's the view like there? Do you have a studio or creative space? What are you creating? How does your body feel when you wake up in the morning? What kind of clothes make you feel the most inspired? What kind of food feels the most nourishing for your creative practices? Who are you surrounded by and are they creating things as well? Do you collaborate with them or do you prefer to work solo? What kind of impact do your creations have in the world? What do you do for fun? What kind of thoughts do you tell yourself to support your creative process?

Now imagine coming together for the most incredibly wild creative party you can dream up with your favorite crew of fellow creative beings. You're all dressed to the nines in the most fantastic regalia imaginable, and the dance floor is on fire. You and your people are feeling free, connected, fully expressed, and alive.

Now ask yourself, *If there is one bit of collective wisdom this vibrant group of creative beings wants to share with the world, what would it be?*

Here are some of my favorites, including some that inspired the chapter titles in this book:

- Wild hearts open doors.

- Find flow within structure.

- The magic is in the details.

- Fear is a catalyst for growth.

- Dance between comfort and risk.

- Work with what's working.

Whatever bit of wisdom flows through, write that gem down and put it in a place where you'll see it often. Let this message be a guidepost you return to again and again as you keep the dream alive in your heart.

While your most realized creative life might not be entirely doable for one reason or another, it's important to let yourself dream big in order to discover what's lurking beyond your more rational and limited ways of thinking and being. Maybe you didn't even realize you wanted to live on a cliff near the sea, wear only red velvet jumpsuits, make abstract sculptures out of clay, and eat fresh fruit from your trees. When you allow yourself to get a glimpse of these bigger dreams, you can begin to orient yourself in their direction and start taking small steps forward. On the other hand, if you never let yourself imagine these things in the first place, it can feel challenging to even remember what's possible.

Just like creating those thousand bad paintings, creating your life is an act of perseverance, trust, and letting go. Each day presents new opportunities to wake up and catch yourself from sleepwalking through this grand creative act. You are the one holding the paintbrush, and you get to choose the colors and textures that you lay down every day. You get to decide what stays and what goes—and what gets to come back later in a different form.

I'm here to remind you that you can allow the currents of your life to move you to tears and let those tears turn to laughter. Let it all teach you as you ride the waves of tender creative awakening. Invite each passing year and each life experience to change and transform you, like water carving stone. Remember, it's never too late to make your next bold move.

After all, there are only a certain number of colors on the color wheel or musical notes on a scale, but there are infinite ways to combine them. The same is true with how you create your life. This book is about remembering your options.

The canvas of your life awaits.

2

Work with What's Working

All that will matter, all that will ever amount to anything, is the relationship to the world you carry around inside of you.

—Sarah Blondin

In art school, we did a lot of stepping back and asking ourselves, *What's not working here?* These critiques, as they were called, were nerve-racking, and for good reason. Choosing to seek out and focus on our own faults wasn't fun, but it did, in moments, help to clarify the path forward by illuminating what we could improve upon based on where we are now and where we'd like to be. However, these critiques often had a much different effect on me. Focusing on what *wasn't* working created an environment of comparison, uneasiness, and shame. For a new art student who was learning by leaps and bounds what was possible in the creative process, these critiques had a tricky way of shutting down my free-flowing intuition. I became overwhelmed by my fear of doing it wrong.

It would take me years to discover that focusing on what *was* working rather than on what *wasn't* could unlock my creative freedom in a powerful way.

When I started to teach my painting process to groups, it came as no surprise that most people tended to notice what wasn't working in their paintings. It seems many of us have been programmed from an early age to zero in on our perceived faults, and when it comes to critiquing our vulnerable creative process, we may find even more reason to seek out what's wrong, bad, or not enough. When this fault-seeking lens becomes our default mode in the creative process, it can shut down what's naturally free and alive. From this place, it's easy to feel stuck and self-critical or regress into old patterns we thought we were done with.

When you consider the relentless messaging of multimillion-dollar advertising campaigns that encourage us to buy more by telling us we're not good enough, smart enough, pretty enough, thin enough, or fill-in-the-blank enough, it's easy to see how our brain learns to seek out what's not working. Our thinking gets stuck in that familiar grooved track and barrels full steam ahead.

Focusing on what's *not* working in life can have a similar effect to doing so in an artmaking practice. I, for one, have spent more time than I care to admit going down deep rabbit holes of self-criticism, only to feel worse in the end. Unrealistic cultural expectations, engrained family dynamics, and my own version of perfectionism have set the stage for stories like *I'm not pretty enough to be loved, smart enough to be successful, or funny enough to be charming* to take root deep in my unconscious.

Over the years, I've learned that one stray thread of unchecked self-criticism can quickly unravel into an unruly ball of shame and self-doubt. That's why learning to work with what's working has become such a powerful tool for me in both life and art.

Asking a Different Question

So how do we pull out of these tiresome, endless loops of self-criticism? How do we shift our focus away from what's not working toward what is working? And what do we do once we get there?

There are many moments in the creative process—and in life—when we're not feeling it for one reason or another. We might be tired, overwhelmed, overcommitted, distracted, or experiencing grief or trauma. I've certainly been there plenty of times myself, and sometimes I don't mind feeling less than 100 percent engaged. It's OK to not always be *on*. That sounds exhausting. But let's assume for a moment that you *do* want to feel a sense of creative flow and inspired engagement that brings purpose, commitment, and energy to whatever you're doing. In those moments, try moving the habitual *What's not working?* loop to the background and asking yourself instead, *What is working?*

This simple, insightful question interrupts business as usual in my brain and gives me the pause and personal power I need to navigate through old patterns in a new way.

When I ask my painting students, "What's working?" it often takes them by surprise. It's not the way they're used to looking at, well, anything. It requires them to slow down, step back, and take a second look—a deeper look beyond the obvious list of things they don't like. *Hmmm, what is working here?*

Sometimes I hear people say they don't know what's working on their canvas or they're not sure what "working" even means. If you're feeling this way, try substituting any of the following questions until you find one that seems clearer for you: *What feels interesting to me right now? What feels good in my body? What delights my eye? What brings me joy? What feels like a hell yes?* These are all great questions to ask in life too.

Your answers might not be loud and clear, and that's OK. What matters is your willingness to look at things from a new angle. That, in and of itself, is a huge step away from old habitual patterns of seeking out the flaws in any given situation. When you consider what could be working, it can open up an exciting new direction.

It's also important to remember that what's working from your perspective may be different than what other people around you see and feel. Your favorite area of a painting, or the part of your life that feels the most exciting to you right now, may in fact be the exact thing that your family or friends feel triggered or confused by. This can be especially true if it's something that they're not used to or that doesn't fit in with their concept of who they think you are.

While this can be disheartening, it's essential to orient your sense of what's working based on how *you* feel. This is your life, your great work of art. You are the artist who gets to make the decisions. You are the creator holding the brush.

Another thing to keep in mind is that what's working might be something tiny. In a painting, it could be one square inch of vibrant blue, the dynamic shape of a flower petal, or the softness of a brush mark. It could be anything you see on the canvas that feels interesting, exciting, or alive to you at that moment. I believe we can always find something interesting when we make the effort to look for it.

Once you identify what's working in your art or in your life, there are infinite ways to build on it. You could choose to add more of the vibrant blue or quiet the area around the flower petal to draw more attention to it. How about experimenting with other ways to use that lovely soft brush or adding details to any beloved area you want to highlight? There's really no right or wrong way to work with what's working, as long as you're moving from a place of inspired action and staying connected to what you're feeling drawn to in the moment.

In life, what's working might be one particular relationship or an aspect of that relationship, a new hobby, or a small shift in your routine. A friend recently said that what's working in her life right now is her daily commitment to making her morning green juice. She says that this one small positive shift inspires her to make better food and lifestyle choices throughout the rest of the day.

About a year ago, I started charging my phone in my kitchen instead of in my bedroom overnight. I purchased a new alarm clock that gently nudges me awake by filling my bedroom with sunrise colors and birdsong, which in and of itself was an awesome upgrade to my blaring phone alarm. Beyond that, having my phone in a different room inspired me to read more, wind down naturally, and go to bed earlier. In the morning, I got in the habit of stretching and meditating before doing anything else, because my phone wasn't within arm's reach.

When I realized how well that little shift of giving myself some phone space was working, I decided to work with it by giving myself more time away from technology throughout the day. I purposefully started to leave my phone at home when I went out with friends or took my morning walk. And sure enough, these simple shifts led me to more of what my soul was really craving: more connection to myself, my wellness, the people I love, nature, and the present moment. *Voilà.*

Try This On

Think of an area in your life where you're craving some change. It could be your health, a friendship, your love life, your home, work, creativity, or any place that could use some loving attention. Instead of focusing on what's not working in that area, try asking yourself what is already working. Remember, this could be one very small aspect of the situation. In your journal, write about what's working and brainstorm creative ways to take that further. In other words, how could you use the momentum of the good stuff to inspire more positive shifts in that direction?

For example, if you're bored with how your house looks and feels but you love the light that pours through one window, arrange your furniture and plants to take full advantage of those light-filled moments. If you're struggling with your creative process but you find peace in casually taking pictures, create a photo scavenger hunt in your neighborhood.

Savoring and Celebrating

Taking the time to reflect on what's already working for you not only keeps you from circling the drain of negativity, it also reminds you to appreciate the blessings in your life right now. In this way, working with what's working becomes a type of gratitude practice. The more you acknowledge and cheer on the seeds of possibility, the more they grow and bloom, perhaps in ways you can't even imagine.

This is also why I try to notice and celebrate *moments of arrival*. It's so easy to let big milestones slip through the cracks, especially when you're already onto the next big thing. As creatives, we often find ourselves in a state of endless visioning and manifesting, but this might not always be in our best interest. When we tend toward always creating new, better, faster, more amazing things, we can fall into a kind of addiction to forward movement that keeps us running on a hamster wheel of never-ending hard work. Speaking from experience, this leads to burnout.

So how do you avoid running yourself into the ground, while also pursuing your goals? For starters, savor the fruits of your creative labors. Remember to take a moment—or a week—to saunter your way across the beautiful finish line you worked so hard to get to. Revel in the hard work it took you to arrive, and take a bow, my friend. Celebrate what's working, embrace it fully, and trust that your next big goal awaits.

When you get in the habit of acknowledging what's working, you are telling the Universe, *Hey, I'm noticing what's going well here. I'm choosing to lean into it. I'm pulling myself into alignment with what I'm craving more of.* More often than not, I find the Universe responds to this kind of gratitude by sending more of what's working your way.

Turning your attention toward what's already working instead of dwelling endlessly on what's not or fixating on what's up next is a revolutionary act. With so much emphasis in our capitalistic culture on climbing ladders and reaching the next big goal, we rarely hear people pause to enjoy and reflect on all the things that are already going well. It might even feel gluttonous or arrogant. I think it's just the opposite. When we take time to celebrate and savor, we are declaring our worthiness and enoughness, which is both a radical act of self-acceptance and a powerful step in the direction of our own aliveness.

If that sounds like a big task, here's some good news: it often takes just a slight shift in perspective to begin working with what's working.

What's Working in Relationships

This idea of shining a light on what's already working as a way of inviting more of it also applies to relationships. Have you ever made a great new connection and felt the positive ripple effect of that make its way throughout the rest of your life? Sometimes I think we meet new people just to be reminded of how good it can feel when someone really *gets* us. Or perhaps we need to remember just how life-giving it is to laugh, be supported through a hard time, or discover the way onto a different, more positive path.

It's so easy to fall into habits of criticism or carelessness with people we love. In order to cultivate more of what you want in your relationships, ask yourself, *What's already working here?* Maybe it's the way your partner goes out of their way to consider your needs. Or perhaps it's the way they offer loving physical touch. Maybe you just feel seen and accepted when you're in their presence. Sometimes noticing and calling out what's already working in a relationship and letting what's not working have a rest can have an exponential positive effect on closeness.

Learning about your love languages, as described by Gary Chapman in his well-known book, can be a helpful way to understand what makes you feel the most loved in a relationship. For example, quality time and acts of service really work for me, so when the people in my life know this, it makes it easier for them to show up for me, regardless of what their love language happens to be. One of my friends is so good at asking for words of affirmation (her love language), and her ability to ask for what she needs has, in turn, helped me get better at offering this kind of love. It's a win-win for both of us.

When we're able to work with what's working on a regular basis, we stay current and honest with the ever-changing circumstances around us. This kind of mindful maintenance takes persistence and dedication, but ultimately, it's easier to build a life we love through small adjustments as we go rather than allowing situations that don't work to build up and spill into resentment or betrayal.

Transformation, Not Obliteration

What happens when you let resentment, frustration, and overwhelm build up? Can you still work with what's working when you've reached your breaking point and all you want to do is throw in the towel, run away, or wipe out whatever is causing the pain?

Yep. Let me tell you a story.

I met a woman named Stacey in 2010. She was intrigued by my painting process and asked me if I wanted to join her at her villa in Bali to teach her how to paint. A trip to Bali to paint? Yes, please! (Little did I know that I was embarking on the beginning of what would become a lifelong love affair with a tiny island in Indonesia.) After our two-day journey across the globe, we set up our makeshift studio and began by rolling out a fifteen-foot piece of canvas on the floor. Together, we covered the blank space with a wild explosion of marks and color.

I explained to Stacey that we were activating the surface for what would come next. After this first layer dried, we would add more layers of paint, quieting some areas and adding images to others until the painting started to come together in a cohesive way. These initial marks were just the first step on the journey.

However, when I came back to the studio after taking a little nap, Stacey had covered the entire canvas with white paint. I was shocked by this move, and when I asked her why she'd done this, she said she felt overwhelmed by the chaos and craved a clean, fresh start. While I understood her impulse to clean everything and start again, I also mourned the loss of every last color and mark—the very things that gave the painting its aliveness and possibility. Now we were back where we started.

In life, this need to clean up or start over might look like scrapping your marriage or quitting a job after years of not expressing your needs. These tipping-point moments often bring with them a whole lot of drama and pain, and understandably so. Big change is hard.

Over the years, I've seen many painters get to that very same place Stacey experienced on our first day in Bali. Sometimes it happens after the first layers, and other times it's ten layers in. Frustrations are high, and the urge to wipe away every last mark and start again feels like the only way out of the mess. I've been there many times myself.

But there's another way.

Instead of mindlessly erasing everything when things get overwhelming, try working with what I call the Eighty Percent Exercise. This approach forces you to slow down and look for the 20 percent that *is* working. Then, give yourself permission to cover over or transform the other 80 percent. In other words, it's possible to make some big changes while also salvaging and celebrating the best parts of what came before.

This practice inevitably breathes fresh energy into a painting, creating more cohesion and the opportunity to see things with fresh eyes. It also sets you up to create dynamic contrast between the old bits you saved from the original layers and any fresh new additions you feel inspired to add. Letting go in this way also works in life.

The Eighty Percent Exercise can be used when you need to make a substantial change to move a situation forward. Can you remember a time like this? Maybe you're experiencing one right now. These moments can feel like standing on the edge of a cliff. You know what's about to happen will change everything—and that's exactly why approaching it with mindfulness, instead of breaking out the white paint, makes all the difference in the world.

Before impulsively making a big leap, take some time to ask yourself, *What's working here?* Admittedly, in these moments it might not feel like much—and what's working might be barely working—but I really believe there's always something worth keeping and bringing into your next chapter, even if it's tiny or gets covered up eventually.

Try This On

We are living during a time in which the entire world is being asked to let go of many old ways of operating. Businesses and systems are falling apart, and the word *pivot* is on the tip of our tongues. In many cases, these tremendous changes have been forced upon us without our consent—and for many people, it's incredibly challenging to know what to do next and how to move forward in this new world.

Yet, everywhere we look, we hear stories of recalibration and reinvention. It turns out humans are incredibly adaptable when they need to be. In this time of historic change, the idea of working with what's working feels more relevant than ever before. With so much letting go, our salvaged gems from the past can serve as illuminating guideposts. After all, the seeds of whatever can happen in the future already exist here and now in the present. We get to decide which ones to cultivate on our paths moving forward.

To gain clarity about how to move forward, try asking yourself, *What is still working from the past that I am able to usher into the future? What am I able to salvage and use in new ways moving forward? What's worth fighting for? What am I ready to leave behind? What new opportunities are available now based on all that is changing in the world?*

These are challenging questions for challenging times, and the answers might not be clear right away. Take some time to arrive. It's OK to go slow. Just keep asking.

As you tune in to your options, notice how different ideas feel in your body. Think about one path as if it were already happening and notice how your body reacts. Is there a feeling of calm in your belly? A quickening of your breath? A welling in your heart? A rush of goose bumps (or truth bumps, as I like to call them)? Notice if your body leans forward or backward when you think of different scenarios playing out. These can all be intuitive signs pointing you in the direction of your next steps forward.

As you start to experience what working feels like in your body, take note. These observations can help you get into alignment with that particular feeling or vibration moving forward. In other words, what's working can become an access point to return to again and again in order to keep your positive momentum moving forward. As you start to notice what activities and people inspire this feeling of working, it will become easier and easier to know when you're around people or in situations that are *not* working. After all, veering off your path and noticing how that feels is just as important as noticing what your true path feels like.

Trust the feelings. Your body already knows.

3

Stay Local

Now, the most precious thing there is.
—Eckhart Tolle

I love painting on big canvases. I find it exhilarating to physically transform a blank space that's bigger than my own body into a world of color, line, form, and texture that never existed before. It takes trust and commitment, and it never ceases to unearth abundant life lessons along the way.

However, a big canvas demands a lot. It's a ton of space to figure out. Where do I even begin? What comes next? Where is it all going? What if I screw it up along the way?

In my workshops, I often remind painters to stay local. When I say this, I mean don't worry about figuring out the whole thing right now. In truth, you can't figure it all out at once, any more than you could live through every moment of a day or week simultaneously. Everything has a process. Every mark you make or color you add shifts the painting in a new direction, big or small, and planning many moves ahead will only take you out of the present moment. It might feel like you're making helpful plans, but in fact it will only make it harder to figure out your next bold move.

For example, adding blues will make the oranges pop. Figures can create more narrative. Carving away wet paint can reveal the colors underneath. Turning your canvas upside down will change, well, everything. In this way, a painting is in a process of being reborn, again and again, with every move you make. This is why I often refer to the way I create, what I call *brave intuitive painting*, as a practice in presence.

In many ways, the brave part simply describes what it takes to listen to our intuition in a moment-to-moment way. This kind of deep listening requires a surrender of logical agendas, rules, and shoulds in lieu of our often-mysterious nudges, stirrings, and inklings. In brave intuitive painting, we might follow an out-of-the-blue impulse to add a whole bunch of gold, scrape the right side away, turn that line into the side of a woman, or use our feet to paint the next layer. All of these things are perfectly reasonable, brave, and intuitive urges to follow.

However, once you do make an intuitive change on your canvas—or in your life—you're on new ground. Your next intuitive hit will arrive only from your new set of circumstances. So you are always coming back to the beginning, opening up to the reality of what is present *now*, and shifting perspective as you go. As you can imagine, this is a very different creative process than coming up with a plan and sticking to it come hell or high water.

Plans provide structure to lean into, while allowing them to shift and change keeps us honest and awake. On the other hand, clinging to well-intentioned plans that don't make much sense anymore tends to keep us swirling in the past or grasping for an unreachable future.

Guided by Intuition off the Canvas

So how do we make these moment-to-moment assessments that keep us rooted in the present and undeterred by the enormity of the task? How can we trust that local decisions and actions will ultimately bring into being the bigger picture we hope for?

Over the years, I've learned that my intuition is the quickest, nimblest tool I have for responding to ever-changing circumstances. My intuitive impulses tend to come in the form of a deep sense of knowing that I can actually feel in my body, whereas my logical mind often gets stuck turning things over again and again, looking for a rationale to support my reasoning.

Learning to recognize and trust my intuition in this way has taken time, and painting has certainly been my biggest teacher. Rather than chasing abstract ideas about how to develop intuition, applying paint to a canvas offers a tangible, direct way to practice intuitive listening for hours on end. My intuition informs every microdecision about what brush to grab, what image to add, or what to let go of, and the good news is there's not a whole lot at stake. It's only paint and canvas, so if I decide that an intuitive choice I made was "wrong" or I don't like the results, I can paint over it or change directions. No problem.

Inevitably, when I walk away from a brave intuitive painting practice, I feel much more connected to what my intuition feels like in my body—subtle rushes of emotion, a sense of leaning forward, goose bumps, tension in my chest, unease in my belly, and flashes of excitement become my personal red and green lights. In some ways, I'm just along for the ride.

However, the next time a truly important decision comes my way in life *off* the canvas, I'm able to tune in to these very same signals and trust my intuition more readily.

My friend Orly Avineri likes to remind her art journaling students to remember the birds. She describes how birds never have a blueprint when they're building their nests. Instead, they fly out to find one branch or bit of building material at a time. Once they put a branch in place, they head out again for the next twig. In this way, they build their nest, one tiny piece after the next.

The way I see it, building a nest is a lot like building a life. While plans can guide us along the way, we still need to take one small, honest step after the next to move toward our soul's calling. As we move through our days making choices as we go, we are crafting our reality one decision at a time. Each decision informs the next, which informs the next, and our paths twist and turn in response to every little—or big—choice we make.

Just to keep us on our toes, each step contains the possibility of unforeseen changes to the plan. These wild cards that life so relentlessly throws our way are part of the human experience, so developing a fluid relationship with spontaneity is a key part of staying local.

In my own life, I'm constantly letting go of my urge to know what's going to happen next. Sometimes this is really hard, and it gets harder when parts of my world feel uncertain or out of control. As humans we crave a sense of control, and plans can make us feel safe. But if we're totally honest with ourselves, we know that kind of safety is never guaranteed. What is guaranteed is that art and life are always in motion and always changing. The safest place we can be is within the ebb and flow of whatever changes present themselves.

With this eternal flux in mind, I'm continually reminding myself to look for the one next thing that feels the most interesting or life-giving in any given moment, instead of getting too caught up in any one desired end result. In painting, that one next thing might look like softening a chaotic area with some neutral gray or adding energetic marks to invigorate a space. In life that may be simply taking a moment to rest, preparing a healthy meal, or having a heart-to-heart conversation even if it feels difficult. It could really be anything, as long as it's doable . . . the next baby step, the next twig in the nest. Once I make that change, I reassess and look for what wants to happen next.

On the canvas, each decision demands honesty between myself and the painting. If I slip away for a moment, abandoning my connection to what's truly moving me to act in a certain way, I can quickly feel like I'm just going through the motions. This kind of detachment, no matter how subtle, pulls me out of the present moment. It doesn't take long for my lack of connection to appear on the canvas in front of me, which begins to look flat, lifeless, or predictable.

Off the canvas, there's a human tendency to want to figure it all out and have a master plan or to set ourselves on autopilot, but this way of being doesn't lead to aliveness. The only sincere way through artmaking or life is to stay local and take one step at a time, while also trusting, letting go, and honoring what needs to shift and change along the way.

Doing What's Doable

This idea of staying local can apply to anything we are trying to shift or accomplish in our lives. Very often we encounter resistance in the form of procrastination, dread, distraction, or overwhelm. Instead of focusing on the entirety of a project, goal, or transition, we have the opportunity to break down the task to whatever smaller parts feel digestible. Some days might require us to show up one hour at a time, and even that might feel like too much. Each circumstance requires different sized steps forward. For example, you might need to focus on what's possible in the next five minutes. After that, you can tackle the next five, and so forth.

As someone who experiences low-grade attention deficit disorder with bouts of anxiety, working to stay local is essential to my well-being. When I remember to stay present and do what feels doable, my nervous system has a much better chance of keeping up with whatever it is I'm asking it to process. As soon as I pile on too much, too fast, I feel my system start to shut down, which in turn fuels the downward spiral.

Writing this book is a great example of a project that required me to stay local. The idea of sitting down and writing an entire book about the vast topics of creativity and aliveness made me feel anything but alive. In fact, I often found myself wanting to crawl back in bed or basically do anything other than attempt to crystallize my wild sea of ideas into something sensible, tangible, and hopefully helpful.

However, I realized early on in the writing process that I needed to change my approach. Instead of thinking about the whole book, I chose to focus on what I could accomplish on any given day. Through experience, I came to understand that I could realistically write five hundred to a thousand words a day. When I did, I celebrated that mini accomplishment as a success.

As I took these tiny steps forward, I still struggled to reckon with the piles of thoughts and words swirling out in front of me. However, acknowledging each step I made on the path toward streamlining them into this book kept me from crumbling under the weight of the project in any given moment. I also took comfort in the idea that each time I make it through to the other side of a goal, whether big or small, I send a reminder to my future self that I can do hard things. In fact, the only way to do them is step-by-step, with time, patience, and trust.

Resistance often surfaces as you get started with creative pursuits or make other important changes in your life. The desire to begin may be alive and well, but resistance provides an endless stream of reasons for why now is not the time, the task is insurmountable, or you don't yet have everything you need to get started. What I've come to realize over the years is that the change or creative pursuit you've been putting off doesn't have to be the first step.

If you find yourself stuck, break down your next step into something even smaller. Perhaps the first step is putting the words "Time to Create" on your calendar or going to the art supply store, joining a local gym, or updating your résumé. Are you the kind of person who would benefit from finding an accountability buddy when it comes to making changes? I bet there's someone out there who would love an invitation to create with you or help you make the life change you need. Maybe the next step is to make that phone call or send that text. You will know you've hit on the appropriate next smallest step when the excitement rises up in you to do that next thing.

Whatever it is, start with what feels doable and energizing, and the next simple step will reveal itself to you.

Adding a Daily Practice

Here is a story about my friend and her husband who are both artists and how they created a daily ritual together that helped them through a difficult time.

Last year, after going through a challenging period in their adoption process, they were both feeling stuck and uninspired. Wearied by the rest of life, they didn't have the time or energy to paint together or have many deep discussions, but they still craved both a creative outlet and an emotional connection with one another.

Together, they decided to commit to doing one drawing in their sketchbooks every night before bed. It didn't matter if the drawing took one minute or thirty minutes (and in fact they did some of each)— the point was to show up to their creative practice in a way that felt easy and consistent and to connect with each other in a way beyond words.

Once they got in the habit of drawing every night, they began to look forward to this relaxing ritual. They found drawing with a simple pen on paper eased their stress and served as an insightful way to process their emotions from the day. Recently, my friends shared their sketchbooks with me, and I was amazed that each drawing provided a glimpse into what was happening the day they created it. Together, the pages of drawings became a stunning visual journal. It's now been over a year, and their practice of sketching together continues, one day and one drawing at a time.

Try This On

The next time you find yourself wading into the waters of overplanning, rising stress, or apathy, take a few deep breaths and write the answers to these questions in your journal:

- What am I feeling in my body right now?

- What is the smallest shift I can make that will help me to slow down, get moving, or feel more at peace?

- How would staying local apply in this situation?

- What feels most alive in this moment?

- What feels like a full-body *yes*?

If nothing feels particularly interesting or alive in any given moment, remember, you're free to choose! Allow your curiosity to be your guide. Notice what you find yourself doing in your free time just because you love it. Where does your mind wander when you give it space to dream? What gives you goose bumps? What feels more alive than anything else right now?

Taking simple, small steps in the direction of your heart's desires supports you to stay calm, rooted, and open to change. If you want to feel more connected to someone you love, write them a letter or send them a loving message. If you want to be more creative, grab a pen and paper, close your eyes, and see what emerges when you stop trying so hard. If you want to be more active, take a walk around the block or find another activity that feels good in your body.

When you feel inspired to make a change in your life, it's easy to think it needs to happen in one great swoop of a magical paintbrush, but those big leaps often just don't stick . . . if they get off the ground at all. Lasting change takes time and happens through many small steps in the direction of where you want to go.

Try This On

Have you ever noticed how holding on to habits and patterns that are no longer working can feel like being trapped at the bottom of a deep canyon? The more time spent establishing the habits, the deeper the groove becomes. When we finally get to the point of desperation, when we really need things to change, we find ourselves at the deepest part of the canyon, looking up at a thin sliver of sky. How are we going to get out of this one?

In these moments, we're mired in what used to be working. We're a different person now and those old ways of being no longer suit us, yet leaping out of the canyon to the surface is just too much. The walls are steep and slippery, and it's likely we won't make it anywhere near the top. Instead, we need to put on our metaphorical climbing gear and slowly make our way up the wall, one small pitch at a time—staying local, keeping focused.

With each brave move, there will likely be challenges and tests. We may even fall backward at times. And while those moments can be disheartening, two steps forward and one step back will still get you to the top. Even better, you might think of it as two steps forward, one step sideways.

As you climb toward what your heart desires, stay honest and curious about how each small movement affects your body, mind, and spirit. With each brave baby step, remember that sometimes the most life-giving thing you can do is to pause and practice being present in the in-between space. There's a reason they make those tents that attach to the side of a steep wall. Trust that you will move again when the time is right. You get to move, and you also get to rest. You're in charge of this adventure, and your pacing is perfect.

Think of something in your life right now—perhaps an old pattern you want to change—that you've been putting off because it feels like too much. Write this thing at the top of a page, then make a list of five things you could do that would move you in the direction of this greater goal. Start with just one week at a time.

For example, say you want to be healthier. Your list might look something like this:

1. Drink one bottle of water each day.

2. Move your body in some way each day.

3. Eat at least one plant-based meal this week.

4. Take five deep breaths every day.

5. Get eight hours of sleep (or more) each night.

When you achieve all five goals in a week, take a moment to celebrate in some way. And if you aren't able to check off all five goals, don't beat yourself up. Instead, ask yourself if you need to readjust for the week ahead to make things a bit more doable. Remember, it's OK to rest and recalibrate. You're in this for the long haul, and real change takes time.

Get where you want to go by being here now.

4

Begin Again ... and Again

*If you are outgrowing who you've been,
you are right on schedule. Keep evolving.*
—Lalah Delia

After graduating with a bachelor of fine arts in painting and drawing, I immediately applied to graduate school with the intention of teaching art in college. This felt like a safe career path, so I applied to three schools hoping I would get into at least one of them.

Instead, I received three rejection letters.

Twenty years later, what felt like a colossal failure in the moment has proven to be an act of grace in disguise. Without the obvious path of another degree in my future, I had to do some real soul-searching to find an answer to the question: *If nobody else was telling me what to do next, what did I actually want to do?*

I realized that my passion for painting was more alive than ever, but without the structure of a graduate program in place, I knew I would need to figure out how to do this on my own. I started by setting up an easel in the corner of my bedroom and got to work.

Over the next few years, I painted hundreds of paintings (my college professor's voice still loud in my head), and I began to show and sell my work at art fairs and in cafés—really anywhere that would have me.

NPR radio host Ira Glass talks about the gap between that which inspires us to pursue a creative career and the skill required to create something we feel proud of. It can be excruciating to know great art when we see it but not yet be able to execute our own artistic vision. He goes on to say that the only way to close this gap is to stay the course and make lots and lots of work.

Sounds quite like making a thousand bad paintings to me. I might go even further, and say that this gap presents one of the most fertile fields in which to grow, learn, and become more resilient. Looking at it this way has allowed me to embrace my awkward beginner's attempts when I dive into anything new.

When I see new painting students struggle with their inner critic, I sometimes ask them to imagine what it would sound like to pick up a violin for the very first time. Even holding this foreign object would feel strange, and the notes would be squeaky and out of tune. But slowly you would learn a few notes, and eventually those notes would string together to form a simple song. It might take many years before you could play anything resembling the beautiful violin music that inspired you to pick up this instrument in the first place.

There's that gap.

We've all experienced this learning curve in one way or another, whether it's picking up a new instrument, craft, job, sport, or subject in school. The only way to make it across that big open field from clumsy to confident is to show up and practice . . . a lot. There's no other way. The same is true in painting, and in life. Like you, I've had my fair share of daunting new beginnings—those moments when how it's been collides with how it is now and you're left scrambling to adjust.

Going from full-time art student to painting for a living was one of those collisions, and I realized very quickly that it wouldn't pay the bills. During this time, I also worked as a waitress, followed my love of yoga by becoming a certified yoga teacher, and went to massage therapy school. All of these jobs were like new beginnings for me, but undertaking them allowed me to give priority to my creative pursuits by living nimbly and lean, doing the minimum amount of work I had to in order to make ends meet.

I spent much of this period of my life illegally squatting in painting studios and living cooperatively in houses full of artists and healers of all kinds. One summer I even lived in a van and camped in a national forest while painting in my storage unit nearby. Looking back now, this seems a little crazy, but it made perfect sense at the time. In fact, I wondered why more people didn't have the idea of using storage units as art studios!

Time and again, in these years of self-discovery and new beginnings, I found myself choosing the unknown, the untraditional, and the uncharted path. The more I allowed myself to be a beginner, the easier it was to simply show up and give things an honest try. Similarly, the more I let go of needing to know how things were going to work out, the more magic I seemed to experience along the way. Perhaps the most interesting discovery was that the more I trusted in the unknown, the more supported I felt by the Universe.

Although I couldn't have articulated it back then, I see now that creativity and freedom were at the heart of all my choices. Further, my willingness to think outside the box, trust in the mystery, and begin again and again were the same principles I was learning to embrace on my canvases. At the time, I wasn't making these connections between life and art—I was just being me and doing what made the most sense in the moment. But each time I began again, I added an essential skill or new mode of exploration and expression to my life. In a very real and experiential way, I was laying the foundation for what would become my life's work: creating art, teaching, and helping others find their way back to their creativity.

That being said, I want to acknowledge that doing that is not always easy. How do we trust ourselves enough to carve out our own path? How do we serve others while also taking exquisite care of ourselves? How do we begin again when faced with setbacks or failures?

Paintings as Mirrors

One of the things I love about paintings is that they're right there in front of us, staring back and showing us exactly what we've done and where we're at in any given moment. Depending on how we're feeling about what we see, this kind of reflection can seem warm and affirming or confrontational and uncomfortable. Taking in reality in this way is one of the great gifts of beginning, or of beginning again—not that it's always a fun feeling.

In my workshops, I remind everyone on the very first day we gather that being in the room is something to celebrate and to feel proud about. The willingness to show up and try something that many of them have never done before is a brave step in and of itself. In fact, they may have taken the hardest step already by walking through the studio door.

The truth is that most of us like to be good at whatever we choose to do. Being a beginner makes us feel vulnerable and unsure. I'll never forget walking into my first trapeze class at age forty; the potential that awaited me in that room full of mats and ropes and silks was exhilarating but also totally out of my comfort zone. Who was I to think I could fly around on a trapeze at that age? Was it too late to turn around, flee the scene, and pretend this never happened?

It didn't take long to confirm that I was, indeed, the worst person in that class and that my circus-inspired dreams of sailing through the air were far-fetched. However, I was determined to hang in there, so I swallowed my ego and shifted gears. I repeated to myself what I always say to my painting students: *You're a badass for even being in the room. Look at you! How cool is it that you are even trying this?!*

These internal pep talks helped, and with each class I felt a tiny bit stronger. I learned some simple, empowering moves. Perhaps more important, I was learning to cultivate compassion for my beginner self and enjoy the learning process. At the same time, I discovered that I could celebrate my effort and willingness regardless of the results—because rest assured, the results were nothing to write home about.

We all come into this world as beginners, and the only way to find our footing is through showing up to each life experience with the curious and open mind of a newcomer. But this is no easy task! In fact, I think it's safe to say that learning to live is an epically humbling experience overall, but when we add in the sting of perfectionism, self-doubt, and fear, the seduction to play it cool and only stick with what we're already good at becomes more and more alluring.

It's no wonder getting older often means getting less adventurous. That's a lot of falling down and getting back up. But we do have a choice in the matter:

we can choose to stay safe and small, or we can choose to take risks and grow.

Another reminder I like to share on the first night of my workshops is to assure everyone that they will, without a doubt, get frustrated. They might feel like they're failing. They might want to give up, get in their car, and drive all the way home or throw their painting out the window. As much as I will remind them, "It's only paint on canvas—don't make it mean more than that," they will, without a doubt, make it mean a whole lot more. We can't help ourselves.

I don't say this stuff to scare the courage out of my painting students—quite the opposite. I share these warnings to prepare them for the inevitably tricky road ahead. Welcome to the creative process! Welcome to the art of aliveness!

When we acknowledge choppy waters as not just unavoidable, but crucial parts of a life experience, we can choose how we want to show up when we find ourselves there. Will we be swept into a storm of frustration? Will we actually throw the painting out the window? Will we shut down and become unavailable? Or will we remember to take a few deep breaths, recall that it's all part of the process, and make our way toward calmer shores?

This gentle heads-up with my students usually results in a tangible feeling of relief in the room. It allows us all to remember that we don't have to get it right and know exactly what we're doing from the get-go. It's OK to stumble and fumble and start again. It's OK to learn as we go. This is an important part of the process.

Giving Away, Starting Anew

On the second day of my workshops, I do something big. I ask each person to turn to someone else in the room and give away one of their two in-progress paintings. This is no small task, letting go of something you've invested in, and let me tell you, there are feelings! While some people are thrilled to get rid of one of their paintings, others move rapidly through all five stages of grief in order to (hopefully) land at acceptance and hope.

I know I'm asking a lot, but it packs a memorable punch.

Before too many emotions take over, I'm quick to share why I encourage them to engage in this radical act. I explain what happened the first time I ever sprang this on my students in a workshop many years ago. The mood in the room had grown so serious I could feel the frustration, a palpable stuckness hanging over everyone like a dark cloud. On a whim, I made each person give *both* their paintings away to their neighbors. Looking back, it was perhaps a bit extreme, but in an instant the entire room was alive with creative possibility, freedom, and the surge of energy that comes with big change.

The purpose of giving one painting away is two-fold: We get to practice, in real time, the art of letting go, a driving force behind most creative processes. At the same time, we find ourselves with the gift of someone else's fresh marks, colors, and images. With this new-to-us inspiration, we get to begin again and work with what we've got.

Being willing to give things up—whether material possessions, unhealthy relationship dynamics, or other attachments—creates space for new beginnings to take root. Is there something in your life that you're willing to give up right now? Can you imagine how this kind of conscious letting go has the power to move energy and make space for more aliveness?

Once we let go of old dynamics or release our attachment to something familiar, the idea of starting again can feel overwhelming. In fact, for many of us, starting again provokes so much resistance that we find ourselves in a holding pattern—afraid to let go of what we've outgrown and afraid to see what's waiting around the next corner.

In this way, it's easy to get stuck in a kind of unhealthy limbo. Meanwhile, the natural world shows us the beauty and necessity of letting go and beginning again. In nature, we find seeds of possibility, cultivation, new growth, maturity, death, release, compost, and rebirth. Noticing these natural cycles reminds us how exciting it can be to leap into the unknown and start fresh. To me, this is the creative process in all its natural glory—the generative act of assimilating what we have in fresh ways, of bringing new forms into being, embracing change and living in motion within cycles, all while cultivating a willingness to let go and begin again.

In any given moment in life, we're presented with an array of specific circumstances and variables, just like the marks and colors we see on a painting. We may like what we've got going or we may want nothing to do with it. We may feel we earned it or that it's been unfairly dumped on us. It's likely that we're somewhere in between. Regardless of our personal preference, we have a choice about how we move forward. We don't have to fear new beginnings.

In my workshops, each person gets to decide how much and in what ways they will change the painting they were gifted. In many cases, the original painting becomes unrecognizable. Other times, it turns into an interesting collaboration where both artists are felt and seen. Often these gifted paintings become visible representations of what is possible when we are willing to let go, receive input, and transform what we are given into something entirely new.

We get to decide how much to change in our lives as well. Remember the Eighty Percent Exercise? Once in a while, this kind of big sweeping change is needed, but more often than not making a 5, 10, or 20 percent change is plenty. When it comes to tending to our own aliveness, we want to stay current with what needs to go and what needs to stay. That's how we stay connected to our own conscious evolution.

Discomfort and Growth

If you are a person who drives a car, at some point you will get a flat tire. It goes with the territory. Changing your first flat tire will always be the hardest tire to change. After you've done it once, from start to finish, what initially felt unmanageable has become something you've faced before. The steps are knowable and doable.

Likewise, if you are a person who lives an honest, inquisitive, and creative life, you will get frustrated, overwhelmed, and confused. Why? Because you are out there on the edge of what you know and what feels comfortable, creating something out of nothing, relying only on yourself to make myriad choices that have an impact on the final result. This is a lot to ask of yourself! Just like changing that first tire, walking into trapeze class, or picking up a violin for the first time, moving through life with a beginner's mind places you at the bottom of a steep learning curve, again and again.

Can you see how creating a life that's rich with learning, unlearning, and evolution (aka aliveness) also requires you to lay down your need to have it all figured out or fit into a prescribed box? Are you willing to embrace beginning again and again?

Whether you're changing a tire, becoming a parent for the first time, starting a new job, or learning how to date again after a breakup, there are so many moments in life when you'll be given the opportunity to unclench your fists, release your need for control, and unfurl your damp wings into a new, unfamiliar form. These moments are decidedly uncomfortable, and for good reason. You are in uncharted territory without a map, making it up as you go, one brave step at a time. This is where the good stuff happens.

Plus, I have to tell you: you're a badass for even being in the room.

Try This On

In one sense, life is very short. When I think of my lifetime as a blip on the space-time continuum, I instantly feel motivated to soak it all up and not waste one single moment of this precious roller-coaster ride. This way of thinking brings what matters most into focus, while everything else softens and fades into the background. This is the stuff bucket lists are made of.

When we realize that our time here is short and unpredictable, it becomes so much easier to move through the fears that might be holding us back. You might've felt this way on a milestone birthday or New Year's Eve—times we tend to pause and look forward and back, considering how far we've come and where we want to go. Sudden loss or other traumatic events also have the power to jolt us awake. When these things happen, they can often be an important chance to examine what it means to be alive right now and to make whatever changes we think will bring us more aliveness.

On the flip side, I also believe that life is long, and I find it useful to hold both of these truths together in my heart. When I was in my twenties, my friend Cheryl and I came up with what we call the decade theory. It grew out of a discussion we were having about all the things we still wanted to do in our lives and how impossible it felt to get from our current place in life to that place in the future.

We zoomed out to put things in perspective. We said, "OK, right now we are living in this ski town, working at a bakery, and trying to be artists. But remember, we still have all of our thirties ahead of us to do all kinds of totally different things. And then there are the forties! Can you even imagine what we might be up to in our forties? And how about the fifties and sixties? I'm sure we'll really be in our groove by then. If we're lucky, we'll still have the seventies, eighties, and—who knows?—maybe even the nineties and the hundreds."

Suddenly life felt luxuriously long, like we had all the time in the world. Just think of all the different things we could learn and do with all those decades.

Of course, as we get older, the number of decades behind us grows and the number of decades in front of us shrinks—but if we choose to see our dwindling decades as fuel for what's still to come and not as a bleak reminder that we're over the hill, we reside in a place of possibility and potential.

In your journal, make a list of the decades you have already lived through or are living in right now. What were the major themes in each decade? Is there a word, metaphor, or image that encapsulates that time for you? What did you learn? How did you feel? Where did you go? What did you create? Who was there with you? Notice what makes the cut and what themes you see there. What made it special? Was it the trips you took? The special moments with loved ones? The things you accomplished at work? The hobbies you developed along the way?

Looking forward, consider writing out your desires for the coming decades. What do you want to learn? How do you want to feel? Where do you want to go? What will you create? And who will be there with you? Remember, it's never too late to begin again. Allow your dreams of the future to inspire the actions you take now—and remember, you don't have to have it all figured out. With a beginner's mind and the willingness to change directions, anything is possible.

Life is short . . . and long.

Try This On

Building on the exploration in this chapter of giving away or releasing something, take a moment and think about what is weighing you down, collecting dust, or keeping you spinning your wheels. Perhaps it's something you've been wrestling with or hanging on to with the hope that it will someday make sense again. What would happen if you let it go, gifted it to someone else, or laid it down to rest for a while? What about giving away something that actually feels quite precious?

You can try this at home by walking through each room and seeing if anything jumps out at you to give away. A friend of mine was recently at a dinner party and the host suddenly leapt up, ran to his closet, and pulled out a beautiful designer leather jacket from a zipped-up garment bag. He felt certain that my friend should have it and urged him to try it on right then and there. Once it was on, it was clear to everyone in the room that this piece of clothing had a new caretaker. The spontaneous exchange of something they both cherished increased their bond as friends.

An internal version of this is to give away an idea, a dream, or a plan, while remaining open to accepting one from someone or someplace else. This might mean an actual exchange in the sense of asking a friend to collaborate or finish a piece of art you've been working on, as in my workshops, or even something more open-ended, such as leaving a poem, piece of art, or small cherished item in a public place for someone else to find. You may even try collaborating with yourself: If you're writing a story, for example, and are stuck, consider putting it in an envelope and mailing it to yourself from another part of town, or even another place you may be visiting. Be open to reading it with new eyes when it returns.

Try This On
Is there something that excites you and simultaneously scares you simply because it's new and unknown?

Perhaps you want to learn an instrument, take a trip, start a community project, speak your truth, or change your name. Chances are something popped right into your mind as soon as I asked those questions.

That is it, love!

Try writing your heart's desire at the top of a page and creating two columns underneath. In the left column, write all the fears that come to mind when you think about doing this thing. In the right column, write all the reasons you feel called to do it and all the good things that could possibly come from it. Notice if any of your fears are totally irrational, and cross those off your list. Now notice what's left in your fear column. Are these fears worth sacrificing all of the good things you listed in the column on the right? Are they worth sacrificing your own aliveness for?

Sometimes we see what's holding us back just by putting down on paper all the thoughts that loop endlessly in our mind. If you're still not feeling clear, give yourself grace and time to sit with your choices. Revisit your writing in a week or a month and notice if anything's changed. This is your new beginning, and you get to move at your own perfect pace.

Remember, brand-new wings take some time to unfold.

5

Contrast Is Crucial

*Look at how a single candle can
both defy and define the darkness.*
—Anne Frank

Have you ever heard of Scandinavians sitting in a hot sauna for as long as they could stand it, and then running naked and jumping into a freezing cold snowbank? In massage school, I learned about the benefits of hydrotherapy, or contrast bathing, as a way to invigorate circulation in the body. Cold water constricts the blood vessels and lymph systems, and hot water opens them up, so alternating between hot and cold water pumps fluids in and out. This flushing action reduces swelling and invites quicker healing throughout the body. In yoga school, I learned about the benefits of turning our bodies upside down in handstands and headstands, another way to provide enlivening contrast to the body's normal way of operating.

In short, contrast stimulates and heals—not only in bodily systems but also in art and life.

Contrast brings together two or more strikingly different things, creating a dynamic relationship in juxtaposition or close association. In other words, contrast happens when two very different worlds collide, kiss, or simply exist side by side. In my painting process, I hunt for opportunities to create contrast because I know that tension between elements creates energy, a spark, nuance. Paintings without contrast can feel a bit lackluster or one-dimensional. Similarly, adding contrast to a photo brings it to life.

Thankfully, there are many ways to create contrast when it comes to artmaking. I personally love to add quiet spaces next to more activated areas, vary the scale of my shapes and marks, push light colors next to dark colors, pop warm colors (like reds and oranges) next to cool colors (like blues and greens), and build up contrasting textures. Sometimes slowing down, speeding up, switching hands, or changing the music I'm listening to has the power to create a palpable contrast in the energy of a painting. The possibilities are endless.

I often find myself naturally working with contrast from an intuitive place in my artwork, but it can also get me out of feeling stuck, uninspired, or disconnected. Looking for ways to illuminate my path forward on a canvas, I ask myself the simple question, *How can I create contrast here?*

The answer might be to turn my painting upside down, paint with something totally different, like a cob of corn, or add some rich, dark colors. It could be anything, as long as it feels fresh, different, and authentically interesting in the moment. Even if the changes I make don't look good or fix whatever problem I'm having, they breathe new energy into the painting. They serve their purpose by interrupting a pattern that is no longer working.

It's also important to remember that too much contrast might create chaos in a way that can feel unsettling or confusing. Striking that delicate balance between enough contrast but not too much creates harmony in a piece of art, while still allowing it to feel energetic and alive.

As you can imagine, the power of contrast can shake things up in life, too. When I'm feeling stuck, I find it's a sign that I need to mix it up by doing something different. Whether it's an unhealthy relationship dynamic, the mundane routine of a job, or the stagnant feel of a physical space, seeking out ways to create contrast shines a creative light on what is no longer working.

Ask yourself the simple question, *How can I create contrast here?* Your answers are clues to your aliveness.

Hanging Out in Midtown

Over the years, I've had the great honor of watching many people pick up a paintbrush for the first time, and I've noticed an interesting tendency. Despite my encouragement to embrace and incorporate contrasting elements in their work, new painters tend to avoid them. Instead, they stay in what my friend and collaborator Lynzee Lynx likes to call "midtown."

Why is it so hard to embrace contrast? Why do we choose to hang out in midtown?

I believe this natural tendency to stay in the middle ultimately stems from a fear of being too much, rocking the boat, or eventually failing in a bigger, more obvious way. I bet you know from experience that this is true in life as well.

We all have a natural desire to feel safe and in control, and the spark that comes with embracing contrast or mixing things up in life can make us feel vulnerable because it forces us to change and adapt. We'd rather succeed and fail on a small scale than put ourselves out on a limb for bigger risks, even if it means we'll miss the chance at a bigger reward. To protect against any potential wild cards, we avoid anything that might disturb the peace by choosing the middle road, which can feel like the most well-worn and safe way forward.

What are you giving up to ensure this perceived safety? Are you really willing to trade in your own brilliant boldness for the comfort of . . . comfort? What about the nagging unease you sometimes feel, the sense that doing things out of habit and conditioning will keep you stuck in a place you've outgrown long ago and no longer belong in? Would you choose that life for someone you love dearly? Why are you choosing it for yourself? When we look closer and get honest with ourselves, we see the fatal flaw here.

I'm sure you've found yourself in midtown in life before. Or maybe you're there right now. Just as in the creative process, there are many reasons we end up feeling stuck, uninspired, or disconnected. But not to worry. There are many fun and joyful ways to break free.

Inviting Contrast

The first step is to sort through the arenas of your life—relationships, work, health, spirituality, family, etc.—and feel into what's not quite right. At any given time, one area might be overflowing with flowers and gemstones while another contains only discarded and broken parts and pieces. Perhaps yet another area is falling apart at the seams.

Turn your loving attention to these tattered places first.

Once you identify these neglected parts of your life, ask yourself, *How can I create contrast here?* Keep in mind this question might shed light on what is missing, but it also might show you where in your life you could use a little pruning or simplifying.

Remember, inviting contrast simply means looking for ways to create variation and change. For example, if some of your friendships lack the level of deep connection and honesty you crave, consider how you might create contrast. You certainly could seek out new connections outside of your usual circles, but you could also invite the friends you already have to interact and connect in new ways.

I have a girlfriend who loves to create themed dinner parties that revolve around a prompt or a question, such as, *What life lesson did you learn the hard way?* or *If you could have any superpower, what would it be?* She loves the intimacy and depth that's created when the people she loves are forced out of day-to-day chatter and into more specific, connected, and often vulnerable ways of interacting. She also encourages her friends to show up with the intention of listening deeply and asking more questions.

Since most of us are creatures of habit, this kind of conscious deepening between humans often requires somebody to be brave enough to stir the pot in new creative ways. Another way to do that might be to create a special event, plan a trip, or take a class together that teaches something new to everyone in the group.

Can you think of other ways to invite deeper connections with your communities? I invite you to be the pot-stirrer and have fun with it along the way!

Another thing my friends and I love to do is have clothing exchanges. We each look through our closets to find clothes we're ready to pass on, then we gather with food and wine for the big exchange. At one recent gathering, our group started by sitting in a circle and sharing a little bit about our personal style and what we were ready to let go of or invite more of into our wardrobe. Some friends who typically wear neutral colors shared that they were feeling bored by their monochromatic closet and ready to add in more color. Others craved more feminine pieces or clothing that didn't hide their curves. Still others wanted clothes that felt more comfortable and softer. Sharing our intentions and the ways we were looking to change was key, because as we started making our way through the piles, we knew what each person was seeking. This added a fun element of being able to find the perfect piece for a friend. By the end of the night, we all left with bags of new (free!) clothes and the excitement that comes with spicing up a wardrobe.

Remember, inviting more contrast into your life doesn't need to be complicated or overwhelming. It can be as simple as wearing a new color or interacting in a new way. The changes don't need to be monumental. They just need to be different.

Contrast can also enrich our internal emotional and spiritual landscapes. My friend Cvita Mamic, who works with plant medicine and somatic therapy, reminds me to embrace the full spectrum of my emotions. We will explore this more in upcoming chapters, but for now I want to invite you to a different perspective on difficult emotions. It's easy to want to avoid or suppress emotions such as anger, grief, and sadness, but Cvita points out that the more we are able to fully access, experience, and express these emotions, the more open we become to the seemingly opposite emotions such as joy, compassion, and inner peace. When we shut down some emotions, we limit our ability to fully experience others.

She sees this emotional spectrum spanning two sides of an infinity symbol, and she calls the point where they come together the diamond. The diamond is the place where you are truly connected to life, the place where you stay present to the fullness of your emotional life, rather than hanging out in emotional midtown. The diamond is where aliveness lives.

Adding Contrast in Broad Strokes

While small, doable changes can create the contrast we need in our lives, in certain moments we might require more dramatic change to catalyze bold new directions.

In the painting process, we might chase down a breakthrough by adding a whole lot of a new color, scraping away something that wasn't feeling interesting anymore, turning the canvas upside down, or taking it outside. In life, it could mean ending or beginning a relationship, sending your kids off to college, moving to a new place, or changing careers. Whatever your bold move ends up looking like, your willingness to change opens up space for whatever wants to come through next.

Over the years, I've found a few surefire ways to create contrast and accelerate change in my life. Travel ignites the imagination through an undeniable shift in perspective. I wrote a good part of this chapter on a tiny island in Indonesia called Gili Air, and it feels serendipitous to have written about the power of contrast from a remote island that looks nothing like my home in Portland. Every single thing about my experience here is different than home. That's why I love to travel. With the comforts of home gone, we're left navigating new territory and different ways of doing and being. Creativity becomes an essential skill, not just a fortuitous add-on.

I'll never forget the first time I traveled to Thailand. *Everything* was different—the sun and stars in the sky; the hot, thick air on my skin; the families of four riding together on single mopeds; the wildly spicy (and sometimes unrecognizable) food. It wasn't always comfortable, but I loved how it all made me feel: present, curious, and open to the unexpected.

The contrasts I experienced in Southeast Asia and later in my travels to Indonesia and other parts of the world made me feel more alive. They showed me that other realities were always happening right alongside my own reality, a fact I found both comforting and inspiring.

We don't have to fly around the world and land in the midst of an entirely new culture to get the benefits of travel. Most of us have plenty of places in or near our hometown that we haven't explored. When we open our eyes, it's likely we can find many ways to seek out contrast right in our own backyard, by reaching out to new people, communities, and ways of being that we didn't know before. How might you do that in your own life right now?

Another quick way to make big changes in your life is to readjust and redefine your relationship with technology. Over the past decade, I've watched myself and the people around me become entranced with our devices, while simultaneously becoming disconnected from the world right in front of our eyes. We're all navigating a wild west of technology, a place with few rules and little understanding about how we interact with the computers we carry in our pockets and on our wrists. I've felt shocked and a bit ashamed by how many hours a day I sometimes find myself interacting with technology.

How can we invite life-giving contrast when it comes to technology? For me, it means taking full breaks from social media from time to time, creating boundaries around when I check email, and being aware of how many times I reach for my phone throughout the day. Whenever I am mindful in these ways, I feel more focused, less anxious, and more connected to my own center of gravity. The more I do it, the more I'm reminded just how important it is.

Contrast Leads to Growth

In early 2020, the entire world experienced a vast, involuntary contrast to the way we'd lived our lives up to that point. Almost overnight, we were asked to stay home, wear masks, and avoid physical contact with other humans. Many people abruptly lost their jobs, and many others lost loved ones. We all watched in disbelief as life as we'd known it slipped away. Collectively, we were thrust into a wildly contrasting reality from the one we'd grown so accustomed to. Along with great suffering came great reflection and insight.

The global pandemic brought a newly embodied presence to many of the things our culture feels designed to minimize or push aside, including aging, health, grief, sickness, and death. Physical closeness, distance, and disconnection took on new contours and had new resonance. For many, this forced pause and the drastic changes to everyday life allowed us to see, in stark detail, what was no longer working or perhaps what had stopped working long ago. Even though this has been a wrenching time in many ways, I was also thrilled to watch people slow down and even step off the maddening treadmill that had kept them too busy and too preoccupied to hear the call of their heart's desire.

In the liminal space between old and new worlds, I watched as people planted gardens, spent more time at home with family, got quiet, and started to reconsider priorities. As systems crumbled, I watched hearts awaken and new visions come into clearer focus.

We don't always have a say in what happens in life, but we always get to choose how we respond. To me, this is the art of aliveness in action. While the path forward remains unclear for many, and may for a long while, I believe this time is clearing the way for new growth to take root in the ruins of what was and the soil of what wants to emerge.

Try This On

On the island of Gili Air, diving and snorkeling hold an essential place in the culture. One day, I saw a sign at a dive shop that read: WHEN WAS THE LAST TIME YOU DID SOMETHING FOR THE FIRST TIME?

It's so easy to stay stuck in our habits of what is known and understood. Doing new or bold things means opening the door to the unknown, and that can feel scary, even dangerous. Doing something for the first time means choosing to go forward without having a reference point for the experience, and this can be especially daunting.

This is also where the magic of aliveness lives.

Luckily, you can do something for the first time in both big ways and small ones. Creating contrast by making small changes has the power to breathe fresh energy into any area of your life. Can you think of something right now that feels a bit dull or uninspired? It could be a physical space, a relationship, a job, or any aspect of your life that's ready for a little shake-up and renovation.

Now, can you think of one small, doable change you could experiment with to mix things up? Keep it simple and stay local so you set yourself up for success.

If it's really small, get up and do it right this moment. Take the next smallest step. How do you feel?

If you're in a place in your life where you know a big, sweeping change will open space to create the life your heart desires, take inventory of the big themes in your life. In your journal, answer the following questions:

- How are you spending your days?

- Who are you spending your time with?

- What does your environment look like?

- What creative activities are you doing and how often?

- How does your body feel?

Now review the above list and see if this is how you want to be living your life in these areas. Wherever you sense a feeling of misalignment in any of your answers, I invite you to come back to the simple question, *How can I create contrast here?*

Remember to honor your nervous system and the realities of what these big changes might look like. Ask yourself if there are small steps you can take right now to move you in the direction you long to go. If you do decide to make a big change, such as leaving a relationship, quitting a job, or moving, make sure you have proper support in place to hold you through these transitions so they don't cause even more stress.

Ultimately, you are the only person who knows firsthand what is tugging at you under the surface of your day-to-day to-do lists. Maybe there's something right this very moment that is nudging you— or screaming at you from the rooftops—to make a change. Whether it's big or small, acknowledging these stirrings is the first step.

Remember, contrast courts aliveness.

6

Listen to the Call of Your Heart

I hope you will go out and let stories, that is life, happen to you, and that you will work with these stories from your life—your life—not someone else's life—water them with your blood and tears and your laughter till they bloom, till you yourself burst into bloom. That is the work. The only work.

—Clarissa Pinkola Estés, *Women Who Run with the Wolves*

In late August of 2005, I turned on my computer to see images of people in New Orleans standing on rooftops waving flags and clothes with signs that read PLEASE HELP US. Helicopters whirled above as floodwaters rose below. Americans were getting a front-row seat to one of the most devastating natural disasters we'd ever seen. Hurricane Katrina had just ravaged the Gulf Coast.

I was living in Bellingham, Washington, practicing massage therapy and painting out of a little two-room studio perched above a historic downtown theater. I kept my life simple on purpose, giving a handful of massages a week so I could pay my rent and bills, spending the rest of my time painting and building my business as an artist. My partner of three years and I were amicably deciding to go our separate ways. For all these reasons, I felt free.

But I couldn't get those images out of my head. I thought I might get used to it, but every time I caught a glimpse of the damage that Hurricane Katrina left in her powerful wake, my heart swelled and I was moved to tears. Every HELP ME sign made me feel more and more helpless.

After sitting with the feelings of helplessness and heartbreak for a few weeks, one day I realized that my breaking heart was calling me to action. It was a familiar feeling, this relentless tugging and an inability to just move on. I had spent quite a bit of time learning to pay attention to my intuition when I was painting, so I knew what I had to do. Although it felt like an unreasonable thing even for a free-spirited gal like myself, I knew I needed to follow the call of my heart and travel to the Gulf Coast.

I looked at my life and the minimal commitments I had at the time and saw that I could, indeed, make this journey. I emailed organizations like the Red Cross and Habitat for Humanity to see how I might be able to volunteer, and my heart sank when I learned that no organizations were accepting volunteers. There was no infrastructure to support them at the time.

But the call persisted.

So I did something completely irrational. I packed a backpack with a sleeping bag, a tent, and some clothes and I got into a Craigslist rideshare with an absolute stranger. I rode on blind faith, intuition, and the call of my heart right into the middle of a disaster zone.

I arrived in the almost deserted city of New Orleans in late September. I thought I had a sense of what was going on from keeping up with the news, but nothing could have prepared me for what I saw. Empty parking lots full of flooded cars, bright blue tarps strewn over missing windows and roofs, and an eerie military presence permeated the air. This was over a month after the hurricane.

I spent my first few nights camped in a city park where a group of people were serving food to anybody who needed it. Upon my arrival at the camp, I was handed a knife and asked to start chopping vegetables for that evening's meal. The energy was focused yet friendly, and the mission was clear. People needed to eat, and we were there to make sure they could.

That night, I met a few other volunteers who were heading to Waveland, Mississippi, the next day. They told me the eye of the hurricane had done the most damage there, and the relief camp could use more hands. The next morning, I jumped in the back of a moving truck bound for Mississippi.

Looking back, I realize how courageous or insane this all might seem, depending on your perspective. In many ways, it was both. But in the moment, it just felt like what I was supposed to be doing—serving in any way I could and paying attention to the signs that appeared along the way to redirect or focus my path.

As the back door of that dark truck rolled up, bright sun spilled in and a parking lot full of people came into focus. Everyone wore fun mismatched clothes, and I would later find out they all borrowed their outfits from the overflowing piles of donated clothing that continually poured in from all corners of the country. Sorting and distributing these clothes were two of the many jobs here. As soon as I stepped out of that truck, I was met with welcoming smiles, a short tour, unforgettable survival stories, and a list of ways I could help. I learned the ropes as fast as I could and became enmeshed in one of the most beautiful human happenings I've ever had the honor of experiencing.

All manner of drifters, seekers, and do-gooders made up this makeshift relief center. Many of the volunteers had spent time at places like Rainbow Gatherings and Burning Man, so they had come together in temporary experimental communities before, which would prove helpful here. Our other common thread was our desire to help those in need, and the need here felt endless. For miles in every direction, all you could see was the aftermath of the storm—entire neighborhoods transformed into a tangled mess of wood and debris, often with just the cement foundations left to tell the story of the home and family that used to live there. No one had been spared.

I spent the next two months living in a tent in a forest covered with debris adjacent to a parking lot turned kitchen and distribution center. I spent my days preparing meals, serving food, and sweeping the parking lot. No task was too small or too strange. I helped set up a healing center complete with a massage table and herbal apothecary. Our days were long and often challenging, but the uplifting energy of service and community kept us going. Together, we served thousands of meals out of what we called the New Waveland Café, and together we really did make a difference.

After a couple of months, as locals started to get their businesses up and running, the New Waveland Café dissolved. But there was plenty of work still to do on the Gulf Coast. A group of about ten of us decided to look for a new location. My couple weeks of helping out was turning into a much larger chapter. I still felt the undeniable calling to serve; I wasn't going home anytime soon.

The government officials of St. Bernard Parish wholeheartedly embraced our group of volunteers. This parish was adjacent to the Lower Ninth Ward, one of the hardest hit areas of New Orleans, which also happened to be the exact same place I'd seen the photos of the people on the roofs. I had come full circle.

The homes in Waveland had been chewed through and spit out by the high winds of the hurricane, but here, massive flooding had lifted whole houses off their foundations and relocated them into the middle of streets or adjacent lots. Cars sat eerily suspended in trees, and every kind of household item you can imagine was, well, no longer in the house. Looking closely, you could see a bathtub-like ring of floodwater residue on every house about fifteen feet up. The water had stayed there, stagnant, for almost three weeks.

I set up my tent in a parking lot, having no idea that this would be my home for the next four months.

We called our new nonprofit Emergency Communities and gave our impromptu restaurant the apt name of the Made with Love Café. We started serving two thousand healthy meals a day to residents who were just returning to their devastated homes. I became one of the volunteer coordinators, so every day I found myself standing in front of new volunteers, giving orientations, coordinating teams, and reaching out to recruit more volunteers online. I was now on the receiving end of hundreds of emails from people who were also feeling the call to take action. But this time I got to say, "Yes, come, and be self-sufficient!"

One of the most gratifying moments of my six-month stint on the Gulf Coast was during spring break of 2006. College students and church groups poured into the area asking to lend a hand, but our little kitchen could only handle a limited number of volunteers. Looking around at the devastated neighborhood we were living in, I knew those extra hands could be put to good use. We just needed to be creative.

So we hung a sign in the dining room that said, NEED HELP? COME TALK TO US, and a system of sign-up sheets and schedules was created. As volunteers arrived, we plugged them into different crews, and for weeks I watched groups of volunteers dressed in Tyvek suits heading off with locals to clear debris and gut houses. At the end of every day, I heard heartwarming stories of folks forging deep connections with one another and accomplishing what felt like impossible tasks.

I will always remember these weeks as some of the most meaningful of my life.

Toward the end of my six months, I made a serendipitous connection with a local gallery owner who asked me to paint a show based on my experiences on the Gulf Coast. I still lived in a tent in a parking lot and had no paints and no canvas, but as soon as I said yes, everything came together to support the project.

I ordered paints and canvases online, and I was shocked when they actually arrived in the parking lot! A friend built me an easel out of found debris, and one of the residents who frequented our café offered the third floor of her house, the only floor above the bathtub ring, as a studio.

I spent my last two weeks in St. Bernard Parish training a new volunteer coordinator and painting twenty new paintings. These "Katrina paintings" emerged looking like nothing I had ever painted before and like nothing I've painted since. Images of houses marked with body counts, boats, floods, and HELP ME signs spilled out as I processed my experiences through paint. Creating this body of work in the midst of it all ended up providing an extraordinary, unexpected, and much-needed healing experience. The exhibition of this work was one of my most successful shows to date, and it generated the exact funds I needed to move to Portland to start my new life.

Following Your Intuition

I want to be clear that I'm not advocating hopping in a stranger's car, heading unbidden into the middle of a disaster zone, and living in a tent for six months. In fact, I wouldn't advise anyone to do that particular thing. However, in certain moments of our life the call of our heart overrides the long list of logical reasons *not* to do what we're being called to do. I do believe something much greater than ourselves can and does summon us into action. Listening and responding to that call bring us closer to the art of aliveness.

Yet how do we take the time to really listen, especially when the chatter of our lives is so loud? How do we know that these intuitive hits will lead us to our greatest good? With practice and presence and a balance of body, heart, and mind wisdom, we can learn to trust even the strangest and most enigmatic messages from our gut. Whether we know it as intuition, a sixth sense, a hunch, a calling, or a gut instinct, I believe each of us has an inner compass that guides us, even when its messages come wrapped in disguise or are hard to understand.

I often feel a kind of internal tug when I'm painting, telling me I have to make my next bold move. A certain pesky knowingness sits in my chest or rings in my ears, and while I often want to push it away in favor of something more reasonable, I've learned that the more I listen and respond to these intuitive calls, the stronger and more accurate they become. While my intuitive guidance often arrives via physical sensations in my body, we can tap into our innate wisdom in all sorts of ways. These are often categorized into what we can refer to as the four main "clairs."

In French, *clair* means "clear" and *voyance* means "vision," so if you've heard the term *clairvoyance*, you can think of it as "clear vision," meaning you receive intuitive messages through visual images.

Clairaudience can be translated to "clear audio," in which intuitive information comes through sound. (You may be the only one hearing it.)

Claircognizance can be translated to "clear cognition," and I often hear this described as receiving a download or a transmission. You suddenly know something but you're not sure how or why.

Clairsentience can be translated to "clear sensing," which refers to the kind of physical sensations in the body I described earlier. For example, you might notice a clenching in your gut or a fluttering in your heart.

I believe there are as many ways to receive intuitive information as there are people in the world. I also believe everyone can gain access to this kind of inner knowing with practice and attention. It's simply part of our operating system. Starting to understand what feels true for you opens up a powerful relationship with your intuitive self.

Maybe there's something right now that's tugging at your heartstrings, a kind of soul stirring that's either buried deep inside or living right on the surface. Notice what moves you to tears and what brings you great joy; what breaks your heart and what soothes your nervous system. Clues to your soul's purpose are living inside those tears and wrapped in that peace.

Try This On

To unearth these clues, I invite you to try out this practice as a way of giving voice to the parts of yourself that already know more than your conscious mind can articulate. One very effective way to do this is to write a letter from your intuition to yourself. If another word or concept such as higher self, muse, God, or spirit resonates more than intuition for you, please feel free to invite that to this practice instead.

Start by setting aside some time and finding a quiet, welcoming space. Bring your favorite pen and stationery or a notebook you love. Take a few deep breaths to center yourself.

Next, start writing with the prompt:

Dear _____,

This is your intuition, and I want you to know . . .

If you can, begin writing before you start thinking about it. Allow whatever comes into your mind to flow onto the page without stopping, stream of consciousness style, and don't feel the need to edit or craft the writing as you go. All you need to do is hand over the mic to your inner voice, that constant companion and guide who often doesn't get much airtime.

It's understandable that we override our intuitive voice for all kinds of reasons. No one teaches us how to listen to it, it's often quite subtle, and what it says doesn't always make much sense. Even when we do get the message, what it's asking of us might feel out of reach for one reason or another. My trip to the Gulf Coast is a great example of that.

You can ask your intuition to share its wisdom with you in a general way, or you can invite it to weigh in on a particular issue or problem you're having. I imagine it will be delighted to consult with you about your next bold move, and don't be surprised if it unearths some unexpected and exciting directions your life might take.

More Ways to Tap Into Your Intuition

If you're not sure which voices are your intuition speaking and which voices are the chattering of your fears or your ego, I want to offer a few more ways you can tune in more deeply.

My favorite practice is quite straightforward. I make a point to ask my intuition specific questions throughout the day. Sometimes the questions are pretty insignificant, like what kind of tea to drink, but I also make sure to check in on bigger, more pressing matters. After I ask the question, I notice what answer comes to me right away, like a flash. I also notice how my body feels in the moment. Sometimes it helps to rephrase into a simple yes or no question. If I sit with the inquiry for too long, I tend to notice my logical mind ramping up to provide lists of pros and cons.

Over years of practice, it's become easier and easier to distinguish these two voices.

Another way I tune in to my intuition is by paying attention to any subtle synchronicities that show up in my life. Then I notice what I'm thinking, feeling, or doing in those moments. For example, I often see the numbers 11:11 at some point in the day, so I like to pause and see if I can discern any message in those moments. Another way I tap into synchronicity is to notice when certain animals cross my path or pop into my mind. There's a wonderful world of animal sym-bology out there to discover if that interests you.

I also pay close attention to my dream world—or as I like to call it, night school. If I'm wrestling with a decision or question, I bring it to the forefront of my mind before I go to sleep and ask my intuition to share insights with me through my dreams. You can even write it on a slip of paper and put it under your pillow. It's handy to keep a dream journal near your bed to jot down any symbols or stories that your dreams reveal, even if they don't make sense in the moment.

I also enjoy drawing cards from my favorite oracle decks to call up an intuitive response. I ask a question in my mind and bring the deck to my heart to connect to its energy. Next, I spread the cards out before me facedown and notice which card I'm drawn to the most. Almost always, a particular card grabs my attention right away, so I trust that's the one my intuition wants me to draw. More often than not, the insights I receive from these cards reveal new or unexpected information about my question.

My dear friend Rebekah Uccellini practices honing her intuition by offering short prayers or blessings to people she passes on the street. She tunes into different people with the intention of listening for a quick message about what the person needs most in that moment. For example, someone might need love for a broken heart, a boost of self-worth, healing for an illness, or patience to deal with a difficult situation. She responds by internally showering them with blessings through her heart and mind and moves on. I've tried this myself and have been amazed by the specific practical needs that come through and the ease of sending energy to complete strangers.

If these practices sound far-fetched to you, that's OK. We all have different ways of tuning in to our innate inner wisdom. What's important is that it feels in alignment for you. Take what works and bless the rest.

Just remember, our intuitive urges are not always practical. In fact, they often aren't practical at all. When you feel them tapping you on the shoulder and whispering in your ear, you can bet it's for a good reason.

"Don't forget the open path," they intone. "Look at all your options. Listen to your heart. It knows so much already."

7

Move and Be Moved

*The only way to make sense out of change is to
plunge into it, move with it, and join the dance.*
—Alan Watts, *The Wisdom of Insecurity*

When I told my friend Tara Morris I was writing a book about aliveness, she said the first sentence should be, "I am the daughter of Carol Bowley." We had a good laugh and cry over that because we both knew what being Carol Bowley's daughter really meant, and anyone who was lucky enough to have known my mother would agree.

Being Carol's daughter meant I had a front-row seat to learning what it is to be fully alive from the day I was born.

My mom cared deeply about aliveness, although she wouldn't have called it that. She just lived it. She was an early feminist, an out-of-the-box creative thinker, and a beloved community leader. She spent most of my life working at the YMCA, where she passionately developed programs to inspire young children around the country to feel empowered in their bodies and in the rest of their lives. She spent her life lifting up those around her, including the most marginalized.

Carol taught me from an early age that trying and failing were always better than not trying at all. She taught me to feel the fear and do it anyway, and that doing it my way was almost always the best way. Carol taught me how to be a lifelong learner, even when that meant facing the challenge of beginning again and again. She taught me that some rules were meant to be broken and that staying honest with myself was always more important than following the crowd.

Ultimately, Carol taught me how to care for myself and for the world around me and that this was what life was all about. A recent Mother's Day fell on the anniversary of the day my mom passed away. As it came and went, the day carried even more of the tender ache I have come to expect on this day meant to celebrate motherhood.

For the first couple of years after my mom's passing, I spent the weeks leading up to Mother's Day in a cloud of resistance and uncertainty about what the day might hold. When it arrived, I would make a post on social media in honor of my mom, which usually brought up some tears. Then I would gather myself together, push my emotions down, and try not to think about how deeply I missed her. I knew on some level I was avoiding the river of grief that flowed beneath the surface of the day, but I worried that if I released the dam, the heartache would sweep me away into an endless, turbulent ocean.

If you know grief, maybe you know this ocean too.

Where I grew up, in the middle of the United States, we shared a tendency to keep it all in and carry on. In fact, most of the people I grew up around carried a certain amount of pride in their ability to *not* show emotion. As a sensitive and empathic child, I learned to keep my feelings, most of all the hard ones, under wraps from an early age.

However, as I grew older and eventually moved to the West Coast, I found myself drawn to people who were sensitive like me, but who'd developed an intimate connection to their emotional bodies. These relationships became a key part of reprogramming some of the unhelpful emotional repression of my childhood. Eventually I found myself surrounded by a web of souls who cried easily, hugged generously, and could spend hours processing deep internal experiences.

Yet even though I seek them out, these spaces of emotional transparency can still feel a little uncomfortable for me. Giving my feelings so much, well, *space* feels both awkward and awesome. It doesn't come naturally, but I still find myself choosing to stay open with my feelings over and over again. Every time I do, without fail, I feel lighter and more alive. On the occasions that I still stuff things down, I can feel it right away: a heaviness in my chest, the pressure of tears trapped inside with nowhere to go.

However, when it came to the loss of my mom, letting myself sink into the enormous waves of grief felt impossible, even dangerous. I would be a toy sailboat in a raging sea, and I felt sure I would splinter into pieces and sink.

When I think of the wisdom of our emotions, I see it in relation to what we block or what we allow to move and flow. It's a kind of paradox, because we often tell ourselves that if we fully feel certain powerful emotions, they will sweep us away. This was my lingering worry about the feelings of losing my mother. Anger will smash us, grief will drown us, fear and anxiety will wear us to the bone. To avoid this fate, we clamp down, hold it in, and try to soldier on.

It helps to remember that emotions are not the same as the behaviors we associate with them. Emotions only exist as bodily sensations. When we allow them to move through our bodies, we can release them. No matter how painful that process is in the moment, no emotion can kill or maim us. On the other hand, holding on to an emotion without letting it move and flow can lead to stagnation, disease, and addiction. These *can* kill us in the long term. If we instead grant our emotions flow and movement, we can allow the sensations to come and go. In my experience, moving through difficult emotions in a deep way brings us profound gifts on the other side.

Fast-forward to Mother's Day 2020, and once again, I felt the dreaded day inching closer. But something seemed different this year. Maybe it was quarantine and the honesty and intimacy that had come with a slower pace and fewer distractions. I'm not sure. But this time around, I felt a deep longing to step into that river of grief and give myself over to what it needed to show me. I wanted to feel it all—to move and be moved.

I ended up spending most of the day in my studio, alone. I painted, danced, wailed in a pile on the ground, and repeated this sweaty, teary cycle for hours on end. It was painful and heart-opening all at the same time, and by the end of the day I felt cleansed and alive. I also felt deeply connected to the spirit of my mama. Fully expressing my grief brought gratitude, spaciousness, and connection.

What if we begin to see emotions in motion? What if grief can move through us into gratitude? What if fear, anxiety, and anger all have a place in this movement landscape? Over the years, I've learned that *emotion* means my truth would like to be set *in motion*—that is, to be fully felt and experienced on a somatic level so that I can touch and feel all the raggedy and smooth edges, lean into the lessons, and release the emotions when the time is right.

Sometimes that looks like dancing, singing, and wailing, as it did on this past Mother's Day, but other times it looks like drawing slow, deep breaths, burying my hands in the soil, or delighting in a barefoot walk on the beach. Often, it looks like painting. Whatever I choose to do, the most important part of it is giving myself the space to move and be moved.

It's no surprise to me that creating large works of art, playing music, practicing yoga, spending time in nature, and immersing myself in water are some of the most dependable ways I know to connect with my own aliveness. Physical movement creates energy, and when I join that energy with the willingness to feel deeply, I strengthen the bond between myself and what makes me feel the most alive.

I simply need to put myself in the way of aliveness, and let the art of living move me.

Honoring the Darkness

It hasn't always been an easy or linear path as I've learned to unwind my habit of avoiding difficult emotions. One thing that's helped me become more honest and expressive with my emotions, though, is honoring the value in my discontent. Hidden beneath the ill-fitting jobs, outgrown relationships, achy hearts, and neglected self-care lives a part of me that knows what I need to do, what sets me free and makes me feel most alive. Paradoxically, this part of me sometimes communicates those needs through rumblings of dissatisfaction, longing, and sadness.

These emotions can point to something missing in my life or some part of me being out of alignment.

Sometimes they show up as heaviness, sickness, or unexplainable lower back pain. Other times, my mind races around the same thoughts, never coming to a place of peace or resolve. The dull ache of apathy serves as another sign that something is just . . . off. In the moments when discontent, sadness, grief, or anything in between wraps around me, I've learned to pay attention. There's something bigger begging to be seen, felt, and acknowledged.

For sensitive artists, strong emotions can feel especially overwhelming. But these same artists can channel the depths of their emotions straight into their creations. (And isn't this what makes the most honest and moving art truly come alive?) Countless songs, dances, poems, and cinematic moments come straight from sadness, longing, elation, or triumph. These works offer illuminating examples of how to harness the power of human emotion and use it to grow something beautiful and perhaps even useful to others. The more honest it is, the more easily it will connect with the human heart.

Art serves as a bridge in this way between darkness and light.

While artmaking, movement, and moving my emotional body all make me feel more alive, I still have to be careful to avoid certain things that rob me of my vitality. For example, I might find myself reaching for my phone to get a hit of dopamine when I'm feeling discontent. Scrolling, responding, or checking on a few things can conveniently distract me from my pain, but this kind of avoidance usually just makes me feel worse in the end.

The same is true for the array of substances we tend to reach for when we're feeling low. Whether it's food, alcohol, pills, drugs, sugar, or shopping, the impulse to numb often stems from the same place—a feeling of discomfort with what is. However, when we numb out the hard stuff, we numb out *everything*. We might not feel the pain anymore, but our ability to feel joy, compassion, love, and connection also becomes elusive.

While our habits of avoidance and addiction can run deep (and certainly require professional support at times), our very ability to *notice* them is a huge step toward freeing ourselves from their grip. The curiosity I practice in my painting process can serve me in life as well. It helps to take even tiny steps in the direction of authentic observations or questions.

As I've learned to allow myself to be with the whole wide, wild range of my emotions, I've also learned to pay close attention to any judgment I'm consciously or unconsciously adding on top of what I'm experiencing. For example, I recently went through a bout of depression. For weeks, it felt like there was a heavy weight on my chest and I just couldn't shake the feeling of deep exhaustion. Feeling far removed from my inspiration, I slogged through the days disconnected from everything and everyone. Then one day, it occurred to me that I had not only been feeling depressed, I'd also been beating myself up for feeling that way. I would never ask an injured friend to carry a heavy load of extra weight—why was I asking myself to do the emotional equivalent?

Having grown up in a family that didn't make a lot of space for anger, depression, or grief, when they show up in my adult life I find my internal gremlins quickly jump in and say things like, *Really, girl? Everything is fine. Pull it together. You're good and you have so much to be grateful for!* These internal messages not only deny me access to emotions and my truth, but also to my aliveness.

During this recent time, I shared with my friend Melody that I'd been feeling quite low. As a dear and wise friend who knows about my work, she responded with compassion and keenly reflected that I was living the art of aliveness. And she was right! Feeling angry, depressed, or full of grief is actually a crucial part of being alive. Or, as renowned Buddhist teacher Tara Brach reminds us, everything belongs.

When I am willing to deeply experience whatever is crying out to be seen and felt, I gain more access to the full range of my human experiences. From the depths of grief to the heights of delight and everything in between, the more I practice being honest with what is, the more fully alive I become. The more I allow emotion to move through me in a physical way, and the more I get up and move in alignment with whatever I'm feeling, the more I invite the full spectrum of humanness into my life.

If I'm feeling lonely, I let myself be lonely and I get curious about it. *What does loneliness feel like in my body? What thoughts are running the show in these lonely moments? What does loneliness make me want to run from or toward?* If I'm feeling joyful, I let myself be joyful and I get curious about it. *What does joy feel like in my body? What thoughts are running the show in these joyful moments? What does joy make me want to run from or toward?*

Try This On

The next time you feel a strong emotion, or if you're feeling one now, notice if you are pushing it down or allowing it to run the show. Ask yourself how you might give it space to move and, in turn, be moved yourself. How can you create a loving and safe space to be with what is honestly and compassionately? Could journaling, making art, listening to music, moving your body, spending time in nature, or being with a trusted friend support your process?

When you're in it, ask yourself, *What does this emotion feel like in my body? What thoughts are running the show? What does this emotion make me want to run from or toward?*

Befriending your wavy sea of emotions and giving yourself the time and space to simply be with them, no matter how difficult or wonderful they may feel, allow you to create a more loving and honest relationship with yourself, and thus with your aliveness. This gift also interrupts the well-worn patterns you may have of pushing uncomfortable feelings down, numbing them away, or letting them take over completely.

Writer and spiritual guide Sarah Blondin has a beautiful meditation where she puts her hands on her heart and repeats the words, "I am here. I am listening. I am here. I am listening." I find this simple acknowledgment has the power to breathe space into the present moment and to remind my nervous system that it's OK to slow down and just be with what is. In fact, that's the biggest gift I can give myself.

Counter to what we often hear, it's not about changing or fixing or becoming better. Feelings of grief, loss, sadness, and discontent are not the enemy. In fact, I believe they are some of our greatest teachers. They add richness, depth, and texture to the breadth of our lived experience. The art of aliveness is about developing a deep sense of honesty and self-compassion and from that place becoming more loving with yourself and others.

My mom always used to say that movement begets movement. This makes me think of Newton's first law of motion, which confirms that an object at rest stays at rest and an object in motion stays in motion. With that in mind, ask yourself how you can move or be moved when you're feeling detached from your own aliveness. Notice what emotions feel trapped and stagnant and consider how you might shake it up, dance it out, breathe through it, or simply wail with it in a ball on the floor.

Regardless of what you do or how you do it, when you let your truth be in motion, it will lead you to your aliveness.

8

The Stage Is Yours

Don't ask what the world needs. Ask what makes you come alive, and go do it. Because what the world needs is people who have come alive.

—Howard Thurman

Sitting in a natural hot spring in Costa Rica, surrounded by tropical flowers with an active volcano erupting in the distance, one of my friends turned to me and joked, "You need a new name."

I had left the Gulf Coast in the spring of 2006 with a new sense of myself. Not only had I been living in a tent for six months in the middle of a disaster zone, but I'd also stepped into a leadership role for the first time and had the life-affirming experience of being in true service to those in need.

Feeling on top of the world in some ways, I was also exhausted. I had mold in my lungs and the relentless Katrina cough that all my fellow long-term volunteers were suffering from, making matters worse.

With some of the money I made from my art show, I had decided to join two of my new friends from the relief center for a trip to Costa Rica to rest and regroup before diving back into work and life. Halfway through the trip, we found ourselves in that hot spring—the magical setting that gifted me my name.

My name was Shannon at the time. It was my birth name, and I assumed I'd always carry it. However, many of the Spanish-speaking locals we were meeting were having a hard time pronouncing it. So, without hesitation, I dipped my head under the water and thought to myself, *What's an easy name to pronounce in Spanish?* I emerged and declared my new name was Flora.

It started as a friendly joke, but my two traveling companions adopted the name right away, and for the rest of our time in Costa Rica, I was Flora.

Then something unexpected started to happen. Each time my friends called me Flora, I started to notice how this name made me feel. It felt lovely and verdant, confident and lively. While I'd never disliked my birth name, these new sensations taught me that I'd never felt much of anything about it. Flora, on the other hand, made me feel alive.

When our trip ended a couple weeks later, I moved to Portland, Oregon. I didn't know a single person when I arrived, but after six months of volunteering and all my other life transitions, this artsy, nature-filled, DIY city felt like the perfect place for a new beginning.

My First Burning Man

About a month after I moved to Portland, some new friends of mine started talking about going to an art festival that was also an experiment in temporary community. I'd heard about Burning Man for years, and my interest was definitely piqued.

For most of the year, the four square miles of desert that serve as the temporary stage for Burning Man are wide-open, completely desolate, and windswept. But for a week at the end of August, Black Rock City becomes the second-largest city in Nevada. With the vast white desert serving as a poignant blank canvas, Black Rock City is built out of the imagination and sense of possibility fueled by its inhabitants. It's perfectly normal to see things like full-sized pirate ships and golden fire-breathing dragons full of intrepid travelers roll by on the desert floor. And as the experience draws to a close each year, thousands of people sit in reverence and presence as that year's glorious temple, which took months to construct, quietly goes up in flames, carrying the prayers and memories we are ready to release.

As I prepared for my first Burning Man, I kept hearing people talk about taking on a different name there. I assumed this tradition encouraged people to shed their identity and open doors to more freedom. Having just returned from Costa Rica high on the name Flora, and not really knowing anyone in this new community, I figured Flora would make the perfect playa name, as they were called. I was correct on both accounts.

When I made my way to this ethereal place for the first time, I was struck by its otherworldly essence and how at home I felt there. I had never experienced so much creativity, possibility, and aliveness in one place. In many ways, it felt like I'd found my larger community. I continued to make faithful pilgrimages to Black Rock City, exploding and expanding what I thought I knew each time. But the most vivid lessons I've brought home were a new understanding of participation and gifting—two of the ten principles Burning Man was founded upon.

These two particular principles opened me up in startling, life-giving ways that changed the course of my life.

Opening to Participating Fully

As you might imagine, joining a temporary city of over forty thousand people (closer to eighty thousand these days) built upon the principle of participation means stepping into a different world. In this place, citizens not only look at incredible art installations but also interact with them. It took me a few days to really grasp this concept, because it ran counter to so much of what I knew about art, respect, and ownership. Once I did, a whole new level of play and participation woke up inside of me. The city became a magical playground, and I got to be a kid again.

At Burning Man, I spent my days climbing sculptures, jumping into huge pits of teddy bears (a dream I didn't even know I had), calling "God" on a pay phone (she answered!), catching rides in outlandish art cars, and dancing my way through the night under starry skies. My long-held idea that there was always a division between audience members and performers, between artists and nonartists, began to melt away.

You mean we can all be creators of this reality together? We can all participate in making it come to life?

I'll never forget one moment when I was dancing with a friend, and we suddenly noticed a tiny stage up on top of a school bus right next to the dance floor. Eyeing the ladder leading up to the platform, we realized, in this place, we could get up on that stage. We only had to choose to participate.

With excitement and nerves surging, we climbed that little ladder and found ourselves in the spotlight. This was new territory for a shy, body-conscious girl from Wisconsin, but as we danced and people cheered us on from below, something inside me shifted. In that moment, although I didn't really realize it at the time, I began to believe that I was worthy enough to be *seen.*

I also started to understand that participating made me feel *alive.*

With each passing day of exploration under the sun and each passing night of dancing under the stars,

I found myself feeling more and more free, more alive, and more . . . me. I was diving into a transformation that felt like coming home, and the dynamic blank canvas of creative community at Burning Man made it a lot easier to shed stagnant layers of belief and identity.

Here, my name was Flora.

Embracing a Gifting Economy

The idea was simple. No money could be exchanged in the desert, with the exception of buying coffee and ice, with proceeds supporting local schools. Instead, the organizers of Black Rock City encouraged its residents to give freely, without expecting anything in return. The gifting economy of Burning Man changed me in fundamental ways and opened my eyes to yet another level of participation.

Some people gave away small tokens or trinkets they'd created, but a quick survey of the landscape revealed infinite ways to give that extended well beyond things.

On my second trip to Burning Man, I created my own interactive art sculpture called *A Womb with a View*. It was a cylindrical room, made from a fourteen-foot canvas painting hung between two horizontal metal hoops, facing inward. I thought of the cozy space as a chrysalis and added pillows, lights, and a journal for visitors to leave their thoughts. The Womb became a favorite secret spot in the desert to hang out, reflect, or rest, and I continued to make it for years to come.

I also carried a little kit of stamps and ink, so that I could create intricate designs on people's bodies. They ended up looking a whole lot like really cool tattoos, and I loved gifting them to people who looked a little forlorn or disconnected. It's amazing what a little love from a stranger and a beautiful temporary tattoo can do to lift your spirits.

I also loved to seek out people having incredible moments so I could document them with my Polaroid camera. Everyone loved the unexpected gift of a Polaroid, and it's fun to think of these treasured moments living on through tiny gifted squares, traveling out into the world as mementos from this sacred place.

Beyond these more obvious gifts, my time in the desert also taught me that these were the biggest gifts of all: showing up, making eye contact, following the urge to talk to people I felt called to, collaborating with campmates to build bigger things than we could build ourselves, and being fully present with other people in the right moments.

My trips to Burning Man have all been pilgrimages. For seven years in a row, I trekked out into the middle of nowhere to remember what it feels like to be truly alive.

Stepping onto Your Stage

I returned from my first trip to Burning Man deeply changed, and in the coming weeks I did something I never thought I would do.

I changed my name.

Legally changing my name to Flora was a symbolic gesture for me, and it was also terrifying. I assumed my family and old friends would think I was absolutely crazy, and I'm sure some of them did. However, I couldn't shake how this name made me feel—like a shedding and a blooming all at the same time.

Flora felt like the name of the person I was actively becoming, and I was hell-bent on holding on to her and nurturing her in any way I could. This version of myself felt more alive, more confident in her own skin, more willing to participate, and less concerned with what everyone else thought of her. Flora was the version of myself I had desperately been trying to become for so many years, but like all things, she could only emerge when she was ready.

Looking back, I see how my courage to go to the Gulf Coast prepared me for my experience in the desert. Ready for change, I walked onto the stage of my own transformation. In the vast, otherworldly place of Burning Man, I got the message loud and clear: *If not now, when? If not here, where? If not me, who?*

My experience at Burning Man gave me a renewed sense of connection to myself, my creativity, and my community. Over time, this inspiration began to weave its way through my life at home. The guide-posts of participation, generosity, and inclusion wove their way into my work, my relationships, and the way I moved through my days. I found myself looking people in the eye when I passed them on the street. I created renegade public art projects in downtown Portland that encouraged interaction. I sought out ecstatic dance groups to join in my community, and for years, dancing with friends on Sunday mornings was my version of church. When I started teaching painting retreats, I infused them with the magic of Burning Man, although most people didn't know that's what it was. Eventually, the principles of Burning Man weren't something I needed to trek to the desert to experience.

Realizing you can participate in life in any given moment allows you to become an active creator instead of a passive consumer. We can always remain on the sidelines, full of judgment and fear. Most people do, because it doesn't cost us anything to do that. But you can also choose to climb the ladder, jump on the art car, and give the hug. Can you guess which choice will leave you feeling more alive?

I know that participation feels vulnerable, but I believe that the willingness to risk is what makes it so powerful. You might look silly or get rejected, but is the prospect of failing really worth not living? I would argue that sitting on the sidelines costs us opportunity and vitality, and that's a risk I'm not willing to take anymore.

Remember, you get to choose.

Generosity and Abundance

Like participation, we can choose generosity (aka gifting) in any given moment. While the generous choice is not always the obvious one, I find it tends to be the most life-giving. I often ask myself, *How can I be generous in this moment? What do I have that I'm willing to give up? How can I step aside and lift other voices up? How can I be of service?*

Generosity carries a certain energy to it, and the most generous people find opportunities to give in many ways, with their time, attention, resources, connections, and knowledge. It no longer surprises me that the vibration of generosity is also one of abundance. Giving and receiving live in the same space. Trusting and giving generously open the channels to receive. Yet again, the creative process can be our teacher in participation and generosity. When we create, we participate by trusting our inclinations and sensibilities enough to say, *Hey, I'm going take these raw materials and this blank slate and arrange them in a new way that's never been done before. I'm going to decide that I'm worth doing that because I'm a capable creator, and even if what I create isn't useful or beautiful or even understood, creating something out of nothing is one of the ways I contribute to the world.*

When we create, we participate by generously giving back to the world. Without fail, the world shares its abundance with us.

Try This On

In what ways are you staying on the sidelines of your life? What's one small step you could take today to move in the direction of active participation? Is there a way you could give more freely of yourself or your talents that might serve your community? What dreams have you been harboring but not moving toward?

Are there ways in which you are holding back your generosity? Do you have a tendency to hoard or resist the flow of giving as a way to keep yourself safe or separate? Can you imagine places in your life where it's possible to become more generous with your time, attention, resources, connections, or knowledge?

You don't need to make a pilgrimage to Burning Man or change your name to invite more participation and generosity into your life. There are ample opportunities to practice coming alive in these ways inside every day. Commit to one of these, or invent your own:

* Join a weekly creative group—anything from quilting to singing in a choir can keep you motivated to participate.

- Volunteer with kids or elders, with whom it's hard to be anything but present and generous.

- Participate in your local government by attending a city council meeting or helping get out the vote.

- Ask someone you admire to mentor you, and offer to mentor others at the same time, creating a full circle of abundant generosity.

- Create something of value—anything—and give it away.

With a little creativity and trust, you can bring the magic of the desert right into your office, home, neighborhood, or local community.

What kinds of gifts will you bring?

Remember, you are not here to be an audience member watching the drama of your own life unfold. You are not here to stay on the sidelines of your life or to hide on the other side of a screen. You are not here to keep all your gifts to yourself. You are here to share and generously collaborate with those around you. You are here to wake up to the beauty of your life right now. Look, it's all around you! You are here to create and become.

You are here to love and be loved.

9

Dancing Between Comfort and Risk

Would you like to hear an epic Love story?
You. Healing. From all of it. And living free.

—Jaiya John, *Freedom*

By 2009, I had accomplished the long-held and hard-won goal of supporting myself entirely through my dream job. I was a *painter*.

I had worked so hard to get here, and yet I found the reality of my dream job less dreamy than I'd imagined. When I allowed myself to get really honest about what was working and what wasn't, I realized that I loved to paint, but I felt isolated in my studio all day. I loved working for myself, but I longed to connect with and serve other people.

Unable to ignore the rumblings of change, I started talking about my job conundrum with the people in my life I really trusted. It had been scary to admit the problem to myself. If painting full-time didn't feel like the right fit, what did? After a solid year of contemplation and many heart-to-hearts, a new and unexpected path started to unfold.

It all started with a conversation I had with my friend Anahata Katkin. After sharing my dilemma with her, she said, "What about teaching painting?" Cue the fireworks. It's hard to believe this was the first time I'd ever considered teaching my painting process to groups of people, but sometimes we need other people to point out what might only be obvious to them.

This idea of teaching painting felt very *alive*.

Shortly after our conversation, Anahata shared my art on her blog and casually mentioned that I was thinking about teaching painting workshops. The next day, I had an inbox full of people wanting to take the workshop. One of those emails came with an invitation for me to teach at a place called Squam Art Workshops in New Hampshire.

Little did I know this was the beginning of the next big chapter of my life.

I had absolutely no idea how to teach my very nonlinear approach to painting to other people, and I didn't want to show up and try it out on strangers for the very first time. Already going out on a limb with this new endeavor, I felt a responsibility to prepare myself to share what I knew. Going in blind wouldn't serve the workshop participants, and it wouldn't help me understand if this could be the right path for my creative life to take. So I filled my studio with blank canvases and invited my friends to stumble along with me as I figured out how to share this process. They were amazing guinea pigs, and I learned so much about teaching that day. It didn't take long for me to realize how energized I felt sharing this part of my life with other people.

I taught my first official intuitive painting class in 2010, although I didn't call it intuitive painting. I didn't know that term back then or if intuitive painting was what I was doing. I still had so much to learn.

In a quaint rustic cabin next to Squam Lake, we started with the things that helped me with my own creative practice: yoga, meditation, and a walk in the woods to collect inspiring bits of nature. I gave demonstrations about mark-making and layering with acrylic paint, and we took dance breaks and shared our intentions while the layers of paint dried.

Over the course of a day, large, colorful paintings began to emerge, and for the first time ever, I felt like all the parts of myself—yoga teacher, plant lover, dancer, painter, seeker—were invited to hang out in the same room. This felt both comforting and exhilarating.

Combining these aspects of myself had never been part of my plan, but this merging of my passions and interests felt like a breakthrough. I'd been living my life based on what felt honestly interesting from year to year, and now I was weaving it together into a unique creative tapestry.

By lunch on that first day of teaching, I knew I'd found my *real* dream job, and the weeks that followed provided further confirmation. Within days after that very first workshop, I received an invitation to write my first book, and soon I was teaching my painting process all over the world. From that point on, I stepped into a whirlwind of firsts that have continued for many years, up until today.

I couldn't have predicted that showing up to that little cabin in New Hampshire and sharing my painting process with others would lead to a whole new career. Looking back, I understand that once again my heart was calling me in a new direction, and I was courageous and curious enough to get out my flashlight and go for a walk in the dark.

Comfort and Risk

We all seek comfort and safety, but we know that change and growth push us further. And there is a certain amount of risk that comes with any kind of change. When we trust in it, the creative process can teach us how to navigate comfort and risk to create the art, and life, we want.

Most creative pursuits provoke moments of overwhelm, bewilderment, or confusion, especially if we're exploring the edge of something new or creating without a specific plan. Once in a blue moon, we might flow through a project without any hiccups, but this kind of smooth sailing is the exception and not the norm. The most interesting creative work includes some meandering along the way.

I think of this meandering as a dance between comfort and risk.

There's an electric tension that occurs when we live in the space between what feels comfortable and what feels risky. This push and pull between the familiar and the unknown keep us rooted in what we know to be supportive, while also encouraging growth and change. It's in this dance that aliveness thrives.

When I step up to a large blank canvas, a part of me wants the safety of knowing how it will all come together. I want to feel assured that I know what I'm doing and that the path will unfold as it should. Of course, painting has taught me that I can't actually know what the future holds. I couldn't recreate my last painting even if I wanted to, so every new painting holds discomfort and the risk of failure. Stepping into those risks in a spirit of generous curiosity makes a painting come alive.

The same is true in life.

In the story of my career shift, a force greater than myself seemed to conspire wholeheartedly to support my new path as soon as it was spoken aloud. That's not always the case. In fact, more often than not, we can only make changes in our lives through time, patience, and many micromovements. In order to rearrange what exists now, we often require a gooey period inside a chrysalis—a time of dissolving what has been to make space for what's to come. This period of change often means we have one foot in the past and one foot in the future. It can be a lot to manage all at once, and it might feel like you can't grab hold of either comfort or risk, so what's the point? What's important to remember in these times of transition is that the alternative to growth is stagnation—and stagnation is the opposite of aliveness.

In times of transition, circle back to this potent question: *Would I rather be comfortable and stagnant or uncomfortable and alive?*

For beginners, moments of discomfort in the creative process might elicit a feeling of failure or even the urge to walk away. But for the more seasoned maker, these potentially perplexing parts of the journey can be a good sign, a message that we're on the right path. Keep going. After all, bumping up against the edges of what makes us comfortable means that we are breaking through to something unknown. Practiced creatives know that engaging in this kind of authentic, moment-to-moment exploration requires a loose grip on control in order to stumble, wide-eyed, through the elusive floodgates of true discovery. Without this willingness to let go, get messy, and see where the ebb and flow of the creative process lead us, we remain stuck where we've always been.

When I find myself on creative cruise control, habitually reaching for all my favorite tricks, it doesn't take long to lose my enthusiasm. For me, the creative process only really comes alive when I'm walking the edge of what's familiar and what's yet to be discovered.

It's in this liminal space between old and new, the known and the unknown, that I have the chance to become a true alchemist, to bring something to life that does not yet exist.

Your Basket of Tools

I often think about having an imaginary basket of all the things I've ever learned through my years of painting—all my favorite color combinations, painting tools, techniques, and creative hacks piled inside a big beautiful basket, ready for me to grab at any given moment.

The tools inside this basket were certainly well earned. They took many years of dedicated work and curiosity to acquire, and I'm so grateful I have them when I need them. At the same time, I'm careful to keep the basket *behind* me when I'm painting. I know they're there to support me, but I don't give them priority over my blank canvas. When all my handy tools get between me and the canvas, I'm tempted to reach for the same old tricks again and again. Spontaneity, possibility, and the magic of the mystery fly out the window, and I'm left going through the motions, my head buried in my basket.

Keeping the basket behind me allows me to reach back and grab my familiar tools when the moment calls for that one perfect thing, while also keeping the channel open between me and the uncertain unfolding of my current creation. This clear pathway, along with an open and curious mind, offers me access to fresh inspiration that's only available in the present moment.

After years of living, losing, growing, and changing, we all have metaphorical "life baskets" overflowing with the tools and lessons we've fought so hard to earn. It's likely your basket contains an eclectic mix of gems gathered from battles you've survived, juxtaposed with coping mechanisms and habits you've acquired to keep afloat. Think about it for a moment. What would you find in your life's basket of well-earned tricks and tools?

Of course, it's natural to want to keep reaching for what we know. There's comfort in the predictability of familiar habits and wisdom gained over time. Just like in the creative process, there are many perfectly reasonable moments to reach for the exact tool you know you need. You earned that tool, and you get to use it when you want it! At the same time, remember that this automatic reaching can be a slippery slope.

For instance, have you ever felt like you were going through the motions of your life on autopilot? Have your beloved routines become so, well, routine that there's no longer room for spontaneity? Have you lost that life-giving feeling of excitement about what's possible when there's room to dream?

If you answered yes to any of these questions, you're not alone. Life requires a lot of planning, especially if you're building a business, raising a family, or navigating a big transition. It's OK to lean heavily on your basket of systems, routines, and life hacks to make it all happen. Yet the blank canvas is where life unfolds. How can you keep orienting your attention to that space? I find the most life-giving practice is to find a balance between our well-intentioned routines and the space we need to keep free for improvisation, surprise, and change. We keep our basket of lived experience behind us, while keeping the path of possibility open before us.

I believe this starts with a willingness to step outside our comfort zone, again and again.

Embracing Change

After working with hundreds of people in creativity workshops over the years, I've come to realize we're always in some sort of life transition. The very nature of being alive means we're in a constant state of growing and changing, shedding and becoming. As much as we might love a little break from change, nothing is static here.

Constant change also remains at the forefront of my creative process. Most of my paintings go through a wild metamorphosis before they resolve and settle, and the process of creating in this way offers a very tangible place to practice the art of improvisation and navigating change. For people who like to have a solid plan and be in control most of the time, this way of creating can be a challenge—but it often yields potent discoveries.

Why don't we learn about change in school? There is such an emphasis on finding your one thing and sticking to it, and yet I don't know any successful or fulfilled adult whose path has been uncomplicated or constant. By denying the power and prevalence of change, we miss out on building the skills required to adapt to ever-altering circumstances.

To open up this conversation of change in my workshops, I often ask participants to complete the sentence, "I'm growing through the change of . . ."

Everyone, every time I've ever done this, is facing some kind of significant change. I'm growing through the change of my kids leaving the house, my parents becoming ill, losing a loved one, menopause, divorce, leaving my job, finding a new job, rediscovering my creativity, learning to love myself, learning to love someone else, finding my worthiness. The list goes on and on.

Change is afoot, always knocking on our door —or breaking it down, in some cases. With it comes an invitation to shed old skin and reconnect to what makes us feel truly alive.

Try This On

Choosing aliveness is an ongoing practice, and each day presents new opportunities to choose it again and again. However, past trauma, grief, and fear might make it feel unsafe to choose aliveness. Just like in the painting process, there is a time to reach into the basket of familiar comforts and there is a time to move forward into the unknown. Thankfully, we get to pace ourselves as we move between comfort and risk as we feel ready and able.

When you do feel ready, there are many ways to practice dipping beyond your comfort zone that feel less scary than making a big life leap. Start by noticing your daily habits and consider one small shift you could make that would invite a fresh feeling of change.

For example, when taking the well-worn, regular path of my neighborhood walk with my dog Pearl starts to feel monotonous, I play a little game I call Intuitive Wandering. It's simple. When I arrive at an intersection, I pause, close my eyes, take a breath, and notice where my body (not my mind) wants to go: straight ahead, left, right, or back where I came from. Without fail, my body always has a clear opinion, and allowing myself to follow along for the ride turns a simple walk into a fun little adventure.

When I listen and move in this way, Pearl and I end up discovering new places or interesting people along the way. Just yesterday, I intuitively felt called to explore a new path at a dog park outside of Portland, and we ended up at the banks of a river. Not long after we arrived, someone walked up and gifted me a bag of fresh nettles he had just picked. This sweet interaction with a stranger inspired hours of walking and talking and ultimately making a new friend. Had I ignored my inkling to explore a new path and gone the way we usually go, I would have missed out on this delightful chance meeting.

No matter how busy, scheduled, or habitual your life becomes, there are always ways to explore the magic of the mystery. This might look like picking up an instrument for the first time, seeking out a new way home, talking to a stranger, or taking an art class. The more often you step outside what's known in order to discover all that's life-affirming on the other side, no matter how small that step actually is, the easier it becomes to find ease in risk.

I think of comfort zones as islands. These familiar shores can sustain and delight you for some time, until you eventually start to feel, in your bones, that there is something even greater waiting for you just past the horizon. This undeniable call of your soul requires that you allow your gripped toes to leave the stability of the sand as you muster the courage to swim into the great unknown. Surely there will be some storms along the way, but you'll keep coming up for air and trusting the currents—and your sheer will—to guide you safely to harbor.

And how sweet that day feels when you finally find your feet touching the earth again—stronger for all you've endured to get there! As you become more familiar with this new island, you begin to understand that the place you left behind is actually still a part of you, living on and informing you in ways you couldn't have imagined before you left.

This, brave explorers, is how you keep expanding your life to include more and more experiences, more connections, more understanding, and, you guessed it, more aliveness. There's really no end to what you might discover.

Keep your heart open, your basket of old tricks behind you, and your arms paddling toward the next island.

10

Flow Within Structure

Before you can think out of the box,
you have to start with a box.
—Twyla Tharp

I've been drawn to meditation for as long as I can remember. It's kicked my ass just as long.

Several years ago I found myself seeking more structure in my practice. Nervous and excited, I made my way up to Vancouver Island to join a Vipassana meditation retreat for the first time. For the next ten days I would try my best to sit still on my stack of colorful pillows inside a large meditation hall for ten hours a day.

That's right. Ten hours of meditating a day for ten days straight. Was I crazy? Maybe a little.

Our days began with a wake-up bell at 4 a.m., followed by our first meditation session from 4:30 to 6:30 a.m. Next we ate breakfast, followed by more meditation, then lunch, meditation, tea, meditation, dinner, a teacher's talk, more meditation, and bed. Who knew meditation could be so exhausting!

We moved through this rigorous routine in complete silence. We were encouraged to avoid making eye contact or interacting in any way. Technology, reading, drinking, writing, and really doing much of anything besides meditating were not allowed.

I started making elaborate escape plans in my mind a few days in. *I'll just quietly gather my things,* I thought, *slip on out to the parking lot, and I'll be free! They'll never even remember I was here.*

Instead, I kept making my way through each session, just one session at a time. Eventually, all my scheming slipped away as the busyness in my mind subsided. I don't mean to suggest this happened with any ease or grace. In fact, getting through those ten days of silence was one of the hardest things I've ever done.

Looking back, I believe we were all supported in this effort by the extreme structure and container that was in place to hold us inside the experience. Without the strict embrace of the simple rules, I would have been running for the parking lot on day two.

One of the most invigorating things about the creative process is the freedom that lives inside every moment. Creativity releases us from the constrained tasks and responsibilities of daily life. It invites us to step into a world of endless possibilities, where rules are meant to be broken.

My soul craves this untethered freedom. It reveals, moves, and motivates, this ability to let go and follow my impulses from moment to moment without feeling corralled inside expectations or boundaries. In those sessions of surrendered free-form play I often stumble upon my best ideas without even trying. I get out of my own way, and bolts of inspiration seem to just *happen.*

On the other hand, this kind of freedom is not always so life-giving. When there are too many choices to be made, too much freedom at our fingertips, it's easy to freeze in a sea of infinite options. I think of this as creative decision fatigue.

Whenever I'm painting without a plan, which is how I tend to create, I must make decisions at every turn. What color? What tool? Images or abstract? Tiny details or sweeping brush marks? Quiet down or activate? Let it go or add it in? The endless list of microdecisions can start to feel overwhelming, especially if I've been in decision-making mode all day.

I experience decision fatigue in my own process, and I see it all the time in my workshops. Having too many options has a sneaky way of draining courage and decisiveness right out of our body, leaving us feeling stuck in our tracks or running for the proverbial parking lot.

Perhaps you too have experienced decision fatigue in your own creative process. And what about in life? Have you ever stood dumbfounded in front of endless rows of cereal options? Or felt yourself numbing out as you scroll through infinite images on social media?

With a profound amount of choices in just about every move we make, it's no surprise to me that the minimalist aesthetic has taken hold. And restrictive meditation retreats. When you're used to making a thousand decisions a day—many of them of little to no consequence in the long term—cutting down on stuff and options can feel like a breath of fresh air.

Having too much freedom in your schedule can also wreak havoc. As an artist who's been self-employed for most of my adult life, I'm the only person who tells me what to do. I can show up, create, write emails, and procrastinate when I want. On most days, I love the freedom my life allows me, but the lack of boundaries can take a toll.

In both my creative process and in my life, I've learned that sometimes I need to create structure for myself in order to stay fluid and focused. It's not easy. Even the word *structure* causes my body and breath to constrict a tiny bit. I chose a creative path partly because I love freedom. But I'm learning to recognize that I actually can get even more spontaneity and spaciousness by adding a little (and sometimes a lot) of structure.

Riverbanks

In my painting process, I call these self-imposed structures riverbanks. The riverbanks can really be anything, as long as they limit options and invite focus.

I remember one summer night in my studio. The air felt delicious and it was still light out at 9 p.m. I turned up the music, cleaned off my palette, lit a candle, and hung a halfway finished painting on the wall. I loaded up my palette with a spectrum of my favorite colors and began to move the paint around.

I tried out my signature moves, added different shapes, turned the canvas upside down, and waited for the magic to take hold. I thought, *Any minute now, things will start to click.* After a couple of agonizing hours, the opposite was true. Everything looked forced, murky, and far worse than when I started.

I was all over the place, my efforts only making matters worse. I needed to hone in, simplify, and give myself some boundaries. To figure out where to begin, I thought about what kind of riverbanks felt the most genuinely interesting to put in place, at least for the next layer. Riverbanks can always shift and change, layer to layer or day to day.

I had recently discovered a new paint color called Prussian blue, and this deep, dark midnight hue felt exciting to explore. While choosing this color as a bank didn't mean other colors were totally off-limits, it did provide a much-needed color focus moving forward. Sometimes the entire rainbow is just too much.

In search of another bank, I looked through my sketchbook and came across some quick drawings of trees I'd done the week before. The sketches felt playful and alive, and I was curious to see how they might translate into a larger painting—another clear riverbank.

Craving one more constraint, I decided to carve up a potato into the shape of a triangle. This little handmade stamp would allow me to add in repeating shapes, which I knew would help the painting feel more cohesive.

With this simplified framework of Prussian blue, trees, and triangles in place, I felt my shoulders start to relax. Fewer options felt so much better in my body.

This kind of paring down is also effective in day-to-day life. The amount of information we ask our nervous systems to process is truly astounding. It's no wonder so many of us struggle with overwhelm and anxiety. How could we possibly navigate it all . . . *all* of the time?

As you reflect on your own life, can you think of areas that might benefit from some custom-designed riverbanks? Where could a little self-imposed structure allow you to feel more supported? More free? More focused? Is there a part of your life that feels like a messy junk drawer?

Paring Back

Giving yourself boundaries requires diligence and it often means giving something up. If you've ever done a food cleanse or an elimination diet to find out what is causing your body to flare up, you know all about this. It starts with taking away many or all of the foods that might be at the root of the issue. Once you know that one or two basic foods are OK, you can slowly add things back into your diet and see what happens, allowing you to gain clarity about what's causing the problem.

Just like eating the wrong foods, densely packed schedules and obligations can make you feel overextended and bog you down, but you might not know where the specific problem lies. Plus, when you're trying to do it all, it becomes harder and harder to do any of it well, not to mention enjoy it and feel connected to your aliveness along the way. You've probably heard the phrase, "If it isn't a full yes, it's a hell no." As cliché as it's become, I still find it so helpful to call on this wisdom when making decisions. It reminds me that I get to use my emotional barometer to set my own riverbank boundaries.

I believe this paradigm is starting to shift, but we're still expected to prioritize everyone else's needs and happiness before our own. It takes quite a bit of conviction and looking out for ourselves to protect our precious time and energy with boundaries that work for *us*. More and more, I've started to listen to my body when it comes to making decisions about what's best for me. This can happen in a variety of ways. Sometimes just remembering to have the thought to listen to my body can help me pick up on a clear sign, like tightness in my chest or an upset stomach. Other times, it's a little more involved.

One practice that really works for me is to close my eyes, ask myself the question at hand, and then notice if my body instinctively leans forward. If so, that's a yes. If I lean back, it's a no. Without fail, I get a clear answer when I check in like this, and more and more, I'm learning to trust my body wisdom in this way.

Just like pulling the weeds in a garden or cutting a rosebush back in the fall, we can tend to our aliveness by pruning what is no longer serving us. Our willingness to release what might otherwise distract us from where we truly want to go is an act of self-love, and giving ourselves the necessary boundaries to stay the course will lead us back home to ourselves. This is the art of aliveness in action.

During the pandemic-related shutdown and stay-at-home order, many of our choices about where we could go and how we could spend our days were stripped away. For many of us, this brought our priorities into clearer focus. These forced riverbanks, extreme and unwanted as they were, did remove a lot of the static that comes with the perpetual busyness of our culture. For me, not being able to run around town to appointments, spend time with friends, teach my workshops, or travel gave me time to think about what I *could* do. With so many personal freedoms taken away, how could I find ways to access my internal freedom in this new restricted reality? How could I work with what's still working?

I want to pause here and acknowledge the absolute privilege it is to even consider how to stay free under extreme restrictions. I'm abundantly blessed to have an online business and the ability to offer live-streamed classes. I was also able to plant a big garden in my backyard, take up running again to keep my body moving, and write a large portion of this book during a profoundly strange and challenging time.

I know these sorts of outlets and options haven't been available for a lot of people. And there are a lot of us who are struggling in these unprecedented times. But no matter our situation, we can look for open windows in the face of closing doors—even when doors are slammed shut, as they have been in this case by outside forces beyond our control. Other times, we must close our own doors or create our own riverbanks in order to set ourselves free.

One way to know if it's time to rein things in is to track your energy level throughout the day. What activities leave you feeling drained and what is giving you life? Are you able to let some of these tiring pursuits go? Or are there ways to call in new kinds of support?

Try This On

So often when we want to make changes in our lives, our goals are vague. Getting healthy or being more creative sounds great, but where to begin in the endless sea of possibilities? This is a good time to create some personal banks for yourself.

To bring this idea to life and make a plan that sticks, think of an area in your life that could use more focus and flow. Next, make a drawing or collage of a river. It can be simple. Have fun with it! Inside that river, write down one of your goals. For example, you might write: "More commitment to my art practice." Now draw some riverbanks and consider what kind of structure or boundaries might support your goal. For example, you might write: "Draw every Tuesday. Pen/markers only. Set a timer for 25-minute bursts of activity. Do one drawing every day. Participate in an online course. Find an art buddy and set up playdates."

Here are some other examples:

Goal: Getting started with my small business

Riverbanks: Research marketing strategies. Find an accountant. Build a website. Write a mission statement. Join a mastermind group of other new entrepreneurs.

Goal: Feel physically stronger and healthier

Riverbanks: Start going for a daily walk in my neighborhood. Add one extra vegetable/piece of fruit to every meal. Practice mindfulness techniques. Find a local weekly yoga/dance class.

When you start to feel yourself drifting from your goals, you can return to your banks as a reminder of how to proceed or update your structure.

Like a river carving through the landscape, we get to shift and change with the currents of our life.

11

True to You

The world was made to be free in.
—David Whyte, "Sweet Darkness"

"Flora, I'm just not into all these organic shapes and flowy lines we're supposed to be using."

My heart sank. It was one of my early teaching gigs, a weeklong painting retreat in the bush outside of Perth, Australia. We had gathered in a place that felt like an abandoned summer camp for kids, complete with bunk beds, eucalyptus trees, and regular visits from kookaburras who enjoyed perching on the edges of our canvases.

This was one of my first international retreats and I was thrilled to be painting outside on the other side of the world with a wonderful group of women. But halfway through the retreat, one of the participants came up to me and shared that she was feeling really frustrated with the organic shapes and flowy lines we'd all been churning out. She paused and added, "I'm an architect."

My intention from the beginning of my time as a painting guide had always been to inspire creative freedom and invite everyone's unique personal style to emerge. I didn't want to teach folks to paint just like me. But many of us are hardwired to learn by following directions and emulating what the teacher is doing.

Here I was, creating a demo painting, thinking I was showing different aspects of my process and offering tangible examples of how to create intuitively without a plan. But for some people, I was actually creating tension between following their own creative impulses and trying to follow my example. The light bulb blinked on as I saw how easy it could be for my students to think their paintings needed to look like mine in order to get it right. Noticing this allowed me to make the vital distinction between sharing a creative *philosophy* and teaching a creative *style*.

With this insight, I explained to the architect that what I was sharing was, indeed, an approach to creativity based on freedom, curiosity, and spontaneity. Whatever colors, marks, and shapes she arranged on the canvas were absolutely up to her own inclinations, preferences, and intuition. In other words, it's less about what it looks like in the end, and more about how it comes into being.

When I asked the architect to imagine a painting that reflected her personality, she dove into a description of her kind of painting: more angled, geometric, and organized. As soon as she shared this, I started to feel her excitement, which inspired my own. Both eager to see this painting come to life, I wholeheartedly encouraged her to let go of any shoulds or supposed-tos and lean into her own aesthetic and inclinations.

This invitation and permission to let go of a formula and simply be herself on the canvas changed everything. She returned to her paintings with fresh eyes and a renewed commitment to make the process her own. Creating without the pressure to make it look any certain way felt new for her, and it didn't take long for two stunning paintings to emerge. Bold perpendicular lines intersected to create what felt like an abstract cityscape. Inside the boxy shapes, a moody palette of gray, ochre, and white emerged, with pops of orange and red. The results were soothing and expressive—and nothing like the other paintings under the eucalyptus trees that day.

In another retreat I taught in San Miguel de Allende, Mexico, I remember one of my students really struggling with her paintings. She felt like she was going through the motions and not really getting anywhere.

This woman also happened to be a friend of mine, and I knew she was a self-assured and successful business owner. I said to her, "You're a confident woman, right? What would it look like if you decided to paint confidently? Even if you're feeling far from it right now, could you invite your forceful confidence as a person into this moment? How would that feel in your body? What would that look like on the canvas?"

When I asked these questions, I saw her eyes light up. She could invite a part of herself that comes naturally to join her on the canvas. All of her belonged here. Emboldened, she returned to her easel determined to give painting confidently a try.

I watched as she laid out vibrant new colors onto her palette. Standing tall, with her shoulders relaxed and her heart forward, she started layering paint onto her canvas in wide, decisive strokes. As you might imagine, her new approach shifted the painting in a bold new direction. Her presence and connection to what she was doing fueled this transformation, and she ended up quite pleased with the result.

Digging Down to the Truth of You

Over the years, I've witnessed many painters struggle with their own version of this story. Although the details are different, it always boils down to an internal battle between who people think they're *supposed* to be and who they *actually* are. Sometimes we lose sight of who we are when we switch from one context or identity to another. Learning something new often exposes how willing we are to embrace our individuality when we're feeling vulnerable or taking risks. One of the things I love about the creative process is that it offers a safe place to practice being our true selves.

I believe that my particular approach to painting can be used as a foundation to fuel any kind of creative expression—playing music, dancing, building a sculpture, writing poetry . . . Any creative act can be informed by intuitive, moment-to-moment inspiration rather than by a prescription or formula. In this approach, who you are as a person—who you *really* are—becomes essential to creating. It won't work any other way.

Like the other principles we've covered in this book, this creative approach rings just as true when it comes to creating your life.

When we lean into and embrace the qualities and characteristics that reflect who we are rather than who we think we should be, we allow ourselves to show up. We participate. We tell the truth about ourselves and how we experience the world. We decide to be brave even when we're scared. Doing so makes both the creative process and life more vibrant, authentic, and infused with your own personal flair, meaning, and depth.

This is the definition of aliveness.

It's easy to want to fit into a version of yourself that feels more acceptable, predictable, and safe. But I guarantee that version of you is at odds with your true nature. It's understandable, don't get me wrong. From an early age, we take in a never-ending array of compelling and powerful outside voices telling us to draw inside the lines in one way or another. Whether it's your parents, religious institutions, education, advertising campaigns, or peer pressure, the sheer volume of input from the outside world can be so loud that it starts to take up serious real estate in our inner world. With all these competing voices swirling and merging, it can be hard to know where your own voice ends and where everyone else's begins. It can feel tempting to section off our identity, alternately highlighting or obscuring parts of ourselves to fit in and be successful at work, in school, in romantic partnerships, or in creative pursuits.

It's time to do a soulful excavation of your true, integrated, whole self. That version of you holds the keys to the aliveness you seek.

I use the word *excavation* for a reason. It takes self-reflection, honesty, courage, and conviction to dig down to the root of where these stories were born. However, when we realize what we are consciously or unconsciously trading in by conforming to the expectations of other people, we see that this heartfelt investigation becomes well worth the gritty effort.

In the creative process and in life, it can be tempting to move through someone else's magical step-by-step process, especially if that someone promises the result will be a beautiful piece of art or the perfect job, house, or relationship waiting for you on the other side. There's always a catch with these kinds of neatly guaranteed results. If you give up the freedom of personal expression, you knock the wind right out of your own glorious sails because you're simply not living in your truth. Instead, you're going through the motions—someone else's motions—and while this might seem like a comfortable place to be in the short term if you aren't feeling up to letting go and exploring, it's always unsustainable in the long term.

If you've ever dropped into that timeless sweet spot sometimes known as creative flow, you know how satisfying it feels to move solely from your own impulses rather than someone else's prescriptions. In this place, formulas give way to intuition, trust, and curiosity. And while you might not always love the results, you can trust the truth behind the work.

Can you imagine if the Mexican artist and trailblazer Frida Kahlo concerned herself with painting something "right" or trying to make her work fit inside an established artistic style or school of thought? The entire world would have missed out on so much of her creative magnificence! Instead, her willingness to paint deep, personal imagery in her own way shook up the art world. It's no surprise that her clothing, lifestyle, and political views were also unconventional. Frida understood that she was not only the creator of her paintings, but also of her life. When life sent her curveballs, she found innovative ways to adjust and work with what was working. Did you know that she had a mirror installed above her bed so that she could continue painting self-portraits when she was injured and bed-bound? Nothing could stop her from being fully herself.

When you live your life following the expectations of other people instead of honoring your heart's true desires, you end up disconnected from your authenticity. This severed, disjoined state makes it harder and harder to feel the aliveness that is at the center of this book. You might feel exhausted or like you're phoning it in and never getting anywhere. You might be watching your life on a movie screen, detached from your own story as it unfolds.

In other words, when you don't honor your truth, you sacrifice your aliveness.

Reconnecting with Ease

So how do you get back in the driver's seat of your life? How do you access your aliveness in a way that feels inspiring and aligned with your truest self? In my experience, the first step is to realize when you've lost connection. This can surface as boredom, apathy, dullness, frustration, or feeling checked out. There are a million reasons this might be happening, and there's no one formula for moving through to the other side, but the first step is to take time to reconnect with yourself.

For me, this looks like putting my hands on my heart and breathing quietly for a few minutes. It can also look like dancing, walking in nature, swimming, meditating, or gardening. The more we experiment, the easier it is to know what works for us. Whatever form or practice we gravitate toward, taking the time to get quiet and listen deeply to the grounding truths of our soul often helps begin the process.

From this connected place, ask yourself, *What feels nourishing in this moment? What sounds fun? What feels like a natural extension of myself? What would I do even if I weren't getting paid? What have I always loved to do?* Notice the theme of ease nestled inside all these questions.

It's taken me many years to understand how much I associate success with things being hard. Perhaps it's my midwestern upbringing—or maybe it's just a prevalent capitalist way of thinking. Either way, it's something I've had to look really long and hard at to begin to unravel.

What feels clear to me now is that the impulse to push harder in order to get what I want, as if something needs to be forced or conquered, is rooted in old colonial ideologies that don't serve me or even make sense anymore. Working hard can be necessary at times, and it can certainly be rewarding. However, it can also trap us into spinning our wheels harder and harder, never arriving where we want to be.

These days, I'm more interested in seeking out and tapping into a natural flow of less resistance by allowing what wants to happen. In artmaking and in life, I pay close attention to where I'm pushing and where I'm receiving and gently directing. This works for energy, ideas, images, and so much more. My body guides me best in this arena; I can feel what's flowing easily and what I'm clenching down on. I also try to notice what comes naturally and what feels easy. When thoughts of *That's too good to be true* or *This is too easy* drift into my mind, I know I'm heading in the right direction.

Like so many life parallels, the creative process gives me ample opportunities to watch my need to make it hard fall flat on its face. In my retreats, I often see people putting so much effort into making a good painting that they squeeze the raw life force and human touch right out of the room.

This happens in my own process as well. I can't tell you how many times, after intensely laboring over a piece for hours, a quick smearing of leftover paint onto a new canvas feels like the most interesting and dynamic thing I did all day. To counter this, I often start my workshops with eyes-closed finger painting set to the beat of a great song. This sightless space allows for deeper access to a place of feeling and playing, which almost always leads to more interesting art. Besides, who doesn't love to finger paint?

The more we're able to get out of our own controlling ways and allow our natural and easeful expression to move through us, the more life we give to our creations.

Try This On

Can you think of an aspect of your life that feels like it's been prescribed by some version of authority, whether real or imagined? What does this how-to-do-life-right manual say? What are the guidelines about what is OK and what's not when it comes to love, family, and work? What about how you look or how you spend your time? Your goals and how you accomplish them? Write the recipe you've been given in any of these areas in your journal. It can be as earnest or as silly as you like, using real measurements or made-up ones. Here's an example:

- 3 cups of self-judgment

- 683 doses of unnecessary apologies

- 1 head of perfectly coifed hair

- 59 minutes of worry per hour

Now, next to that prescribed version, write your personalized recipe for success in a way that actually works and, most importantly, feels easy for you. Relish this process, writing things like the following:

- 1 feeling of accomplishment per day

- Deep, true friendships . . . to taste

- A liberal sprinkle of naps

- 365 days of gratitude practice, any size

Are there places where the recipes conflict or overlap? Can you invest more time, joy, and energy in those measures?

Try This On

One of my very favorite creative letting-go exercises is blind contour drawing. The concept is simple. Choose something to draw, such as a plant, a still life, a portrait, or anything that sparks your interest. Keeping your eyes focused only on what you are drawing, allow your pen to move in one continuous line. Without looking at what you're drawing, things will get funky, and this is the idea! Let it be loose and weird and wonderful and notice how it makes you feel to let go in this way.

What I always notice when I share this exercise is the sheer delight and lightness in the room, and what's interesting is how much more *alive* these drawings feel compared to work that's been labored over.

We get to show up as ourselves no matter what. It's our birthright.

12

Commit Fully While Staying Open to Change

Salt me with grateful tears and cleansing rain.
Bathe me in the distilled waters of evolution.
—Pixie Lighthorse, *Prayers of Honoring Voice*

I'll never forget the laminated charts the doctor pulled out during our first meeting to demonstrate just how hard it was for someone my age to get pregnant. I'd always wanted to be a mother, and in my midthirties I realized from a biological standpoint I needed to get serious about it—the proverbial clock was ticking. But after years of trying to conceive with no luck, I decided to put two feet in and try in vitro fertilization (IVF). In this room, I was considered "geriatric." I was forty-one years old.

Listening to the statistics, my heart contracted with fear while my fierce determination revved into high gear. Even though the data was decidedly not in my favor, I knew, in that moment, I was going all in.

Soon, ultrasounds, blood draws, bags of needles, and bottles of pills became my new normal. My belly became bloated and bruised from the many shots I gave myself every day, and my emotions rode a permanent roller coaster of hormones mixed with excruciating weeks of waiting and wondering if I would make it past the next hurdle.

It was exhausting and exhilarating all at the same time, and the end results remained shaky at best. Eventually, egg counts, embryos, and genetic testing led to a tiny cluster of human cells growing in my body. It worked!

Until it didn't.

After a couple of agonizing months of willing a tiny heartbeat to get faster, it became clear that this baby spirit had come to teach me my greatest lesson in letting go.

Anyone who's walked this path knows how devastating this journey can be, but after a few months I decided to step back into the wild, unknown world of IVF for round two. I was emotionally drained, but I kept my faith and two wobbly feet on the ground. Again, I knew I needed to be all in to be in at all.

Ultimately, my dream of becoming a mother didn't become a reality, and the grief of that loss still hits me in unexpected moments. I imagine it will never go away entirely, and that's OK. I understand that the size of my grief is in direct relationship to how much I care and show up in the world. Big loss requires big grief. This kind of heartache reflects my own aliveness, and flows from a love that's even greater than the hurt.

Besides, pushing my discomfort away only lodges my emotions deeper into my body. My feelings need room to move—to be felt, danced with, wailed about, and seen—and, eventually, released and transformed. I move and am moved.

I understand firsthand how the loss and grief of not being able to conceive and give birth to one's own children have the power to make us want to stop living fully. But for me, quite the opposite happened. It took time, but this loss opened up new doors of aliveness.

I'm not sure I'd be able to say this without my many years of intuitive painting practice, which allowed me to understand that letting go of anything inevitably makes space for something else to emerge. This is true even when the letting go feels painful or we don't choose it. I've also learned that when I let go of something, I always have a choice to make: I can focus on what used to be true, or I can accept what is happening now and look for the new openings.

The past few years have brought great, destabilizing losses in my life. I've leaned into these teachings to help get me through. It has been hard. I don't want to focus on the open windows when a door slams in my face. Who does? But like anything, the more I practice turning my gaze to what lies ahead and letting go of what's already gone, the more pathways I lay down in my brain. My choices, on repeat, make it a habit.

It all starts with remembering that I have a choice in the first place.

The Gift of What Is

When I learned I wouldn't be able to have my own children, it took some time, but I started to seek out any open windows. What was possible now that wouldn't have been possible had I become pregnant? For starters, I wouldn't have spent two weeks writing this book in Bali if I'd become a mom two years ago. That just wouldn't have happened. And without assigning "better" or "worse" to any one scenario, I am allowing myself to be grateful for what I have been able to do now.

I had a deep desire to raise children in this lifetime, and yet I refuse to live the rest of my life regretting the loss of it. Instead, I unwrap the gifts of my current reality and relish the new opportunities that appear all around me when I take the time to look. For me, that looks like having time to birth new creative projects. It means embracing the flexibility to travel and being an auntie to my friends' kids. I've also gained a sense of true, lived compassion for other people facing fertility challenges. This road is hard, loves, and my heart is with you if you're walking it right now.

Moving through the challenges I've faced in recent years has allowed me more access to the tenderness of my own humanity, heart, and aliveness. Those are the gifts I choose, on most days, to keep at the forefront of my thoughts.

More and more, I realize just how much magic is waiting right beyond my perfectly laid plans.

Another lesson that became even clearer to me through this process was the importance of committing fully to something while staying open to change. I had already uncovered this foundational philosophy through painting, and this experience reaffirmed it for me on a deeper level. At first, these words seem to contradict themselves. Can we commit fully if we're also holding space for change? Doesn't that imply we have one foot out the door?

I have a different idea.

To me, committing fully while staying open to change means stepping in with my two feet firmly planted on the ground, while keeping my heart open to what feels honest and true along the way.

Plants show us all about this need to root down before they are able to grow up and out. After all, plants are where they are. Once the seed sprouts into roots, a plant is committed to staying put. Yet whatever the roots or branches encounter in the landscape—a brick wall blocking light or a boulder in the way of spreading roots—the plant grows to meet the challenge. At an apartment building near me, workers recently chopped all the large shrubs down to stumps so that the outside could be painted. The fresh coat of paint looked fine, but each day on my walk, I mourned the loss of greenery. Within weeks, two things happened: new plants sprouted up to grab the sunshine around the base of the stumps, and the bare trunks themselves shot out bright green branches and leaves. They'll be back in no time.

Committing fully while staying open to change means showing up with the dedication and desire it takes to carry projects, paintings, and relationships all the way through. At the same time, it takes a willingness to understand that most human endeavors will encounter some unpredictable twists, turns, and bumps along the way.

It's tempting and very natural to arrive with a fixed idea about the outcomes we desire. Humans love to have solid plans, after all. Plans make us feel safe and secure. But when we become too attached to what we assume is the right way to move through life, we lose our ability to improvise, change directions, and stay present to ever-shifting circumstances. Furthermore, focusing on outcomes can lead to losing sight of our deeper ideals or values. For example, we can commit to growing as people and artists our whole life and then stay flexible about what that means in terms of individual goals and outcomes. Looking at commitment in this way allows us to have a strong core and yet remain flexible.

On the other hand, when we show up halfheartedly, or with one foot out the door, our lack of true commitment holds us back from owning our desires. If we can't embrace what we really want, how can we ever hope to get it? Only by showing up and investing fully can our dreams take flight. Even if we do everything in our power to achieve what we yearn for, sometimes we won't get it. That's going to hurt. I get that. But I'm not willing to add onto that with the regret I feel knowing I didn't commit fully in the first place.

So how do you find the balance? How do you show up fully as you surf the waves of change? How do you believe it's even worth the ride when you know it might not work out the way you've planned? How do you commit fully while staying open to change?

Quit Dabbling

In my classes, new painters often hold back from committing fully. Instead, they do what I call "dabbling." They dip their brush into the paint and take a tentative step toward the canvas to make small marks—a bit of green here, a few circles over there, maybe a tree in the lower corner.

I watch the rigidness in their bodies and see how it translates directly onto their canvases. I can almost hear their thoughts: *Am I doing this right? When will this turn into something I actually like? What's the point of all these marks and layers? I should probably just quit while I'm ahead.*

Maybe you've felt this way in life as well.

Paintings created with a lack of commitment often appear chaotic or unsure because the artist hasn't prioritized anything in a bold or confident way. Instead, the colors and marks are lackluster, fighting for attention, and nothing stands out or moves forward.

In the creative process, not committing often leads to a tendency to check out, give up, or simply feel unsatisfied with the work at hand. Similarly, in life, the impulse to hold back and not fully dive in to any one thing keeps us stuck right where we are, spinning our wheels without knowing why.

There are plenty of reasons we get stuck in our tracks. It might even be a good thing, as when our intuition nudges us away from stepping into something not meant for us. But more often than not, fear, laziness, and apathy seduce us into the false belief that holding back will protect us or save our resources.

And that's OK. We're not meant to engage all the way in everything. But when our soul feels called to show up for something, this is the time to go all in, even when we know the winds of change could blow us off course at any moment.

What does it look like to immerse every inch of yourself in a painting? Imagine moving your body to the beat of a great song while making bold, sweeping brushstrokes on your canvas. Occasionally, you dance your way back for some quick perspective before lunging forward to make your next bold move. You acknowledge any negative voices chattering away in your head. They can come along for the ride, but they won't be driving under any circumstances. They don't get any input on the destination, either.

When you get stuck or confused, take it as a sign to get curious. Ask some of the well-loved questions you know will serve the creative process: *What wants to change? What wants to move? What's working? What wants to stay? What am I ready to let go of or give away? What wants to be added in?*

Even if no clear answers present themselves right away, understand that something will come. You're free to choose, change, reimagine. Staying connected to this place of freedom and trust, you add an impulsive streak of deep blue across the top of the canvas, and then step back for another look.

Suddenly, the blue asks to be at the bottom of the painting, and so you follow the urge to spin the painting upside down. The bold streak morphs into a winding blue river, and the image of a female figure comes to you. You add her, opening a new story about a woman and a river on your canvas. You know this scene might stay, but maybe it will get even more dynamic if you allow it to transform, again, into something unexpected?

You see where I'm going with this. Anything is possible when you commit fully while staying open to change. In fact, it's a kind of sweet spot that engenders freedom, honesty, and curiosity. In artmaking or in life, you get to choose what happens next based on your preferences, intuition, and lived experience. If you don't like the blue river, you have the power to let it go or transform it into something else—maybe it becomes the curve in a flower petal, a shadow in the night sky, or a dynamic abstraction.

Each moment holds infinite options when you remember to look for the open windows instead of the closed doors.

Epic Love

Today, I feel an underlying sense of peace in my heart knowing I gave trying to become a mother everything I had, even though it didn't turn out as I had hoped.

Being both steadfast and flexible in my IVF journey allowed me to navigate an otherwise heartbreaking moment with presence, understanding, and the ability to ultimately let go. Of course, I find many subtler moments in everyday life in which the combination of dedication and openness has the potential to smooth rough edges, invite more ease, and allow for inevitable and necessary change.

If you've ever applied for a job or a school and given the application process everything you had even though your chances of getting in were slim, you've committed fully while staying open to change. If you've ever entered a race you weren't sure you could finish, moved to a new city without knowing a soul, or even just gotten out of bed during a pandemic, you've committed fully while staying open to change.

Intimate relationships also give us ample opportunities to practice this. There's never any real guarantee that love will last, but putting both feet in allows us to experience the depths of connection that are only available when we fully commit. On the other hand, dabbling with intimacy or keeping our hearts safely locked feels like the surest way to keep the love we seek at a safe distance.

We can't have one without the other.

Recently, I shared that I was looking for epic love with a person I had just started dating. Pretty brave, right? But as a single middle-aged gal looking for love, I figured, *What do I have to lose?* He replied by saying, "Wow. Nobody says that. People say they want a partner or a best friend, but nobody says they want epic love. It's just too vulnerable."

He made a good point, and the more I reflected on it, the more I realized it had taken me forty-five years to be able to say I wanted epic love—because it had taken me that long to believe I deserved it.

Try This On

The same questions that keep your creative process alive and free can also help you get clarity on what might be wanting or ready to change in life. If you're feeling stuck in your job, or exhausted by a relationship, you might try asking yourself these questions: *Is there anything I feel called and able to do in this moment? What feels genuinely interesting or alive, or even just makes me a little bit curious? What wants to change? What wants to move? What is working? What wants to stay? What am I ready to let go of? What wants to be added in?*

When you ask, tell yourself you'll bravely listen to the responses. You don't necessarily have to act on them, but don't pass up the chance to commit fully to the practices of honest inquiry, creative thinking, and intuitive listening. You have the power to change, respond, and grow in all areas of your life, right now. It can be as simple as asking yourself what foods make you feel the most alive or what clothes you're ready to let go of. Or perhaps it's time to explore some deeper belief systems that are holding you back from devoting yourself fully to your own life.

Each time you practice asking these questions, you get to try on what standing in your truth feels like. Be sure to notice how it shows up in your body. Does it feel invigorating? Calming? Empowering? Eventually, anything less than your truth will begin to feel like clothes that don't quite fit. Over time, your ability to remain in these ill-fitting realities will become harder and harder to tolerate.

This is something to celebrate, friends.

In life, we get chances every day to practice committing fully while staying open to change. Can you think of one now? Visualize showing up, tall in your spine, shoulders back, legs sturdy. Feel a lightness in your feet, a fluidity in your breath and bones. A soft, responsive belly. Can you be firmly committed and fully present, while also being true to your needs as they shift and change?

Draw an image of yourself standing in your truth like this. What words of affirmation would you write across your heart to remind you of what's possible?

Try This On

To practice committing fully while staying open to change, try this simple drawing exercise. On a piece of paper, start by making a few marks. Then turn your paper ninety degrees, and take another look. What do you see in this new orientation? Notice what you feel called to do next, and *do it*. Resist the urge to overthink. Repeat this process a few times, turning your paper ninety degrees every thirty seconds or so, or whenever you feel ready. With each turn of the page, allow yourself to let go of what was and become present to what's ready to become. Commit fully at every turn, but stay open to the ever-changing drawing in front of you.

Notice how this practice made you feel. Was it liberating? Frustrating? Perhaps a little bit of both? Remember, this is just a playful way to practice the art of improvisation and adaptability. It really doesn't matter what your drawing looks like in the end, as long as you give it a try.

In life and in the creative process, committing with bended knees and open palms invites more presence, honesty, and flexibility as you navigate uncharted waters. It may feel awkward and even scary at first, but the more you learn to trust your inner compass and the ever-changing tides of your life, the more natural it will become to occupy this firm yet fluid space.

Don't dwell on what has passed or is yet to be—as songwriter Leonard Cohen reminds us, ring the bells you still can ring.

13

The Power of Community

Take your attention down into the tiny, miraculous stitching of the life you are creating from nothing, and trust that each small thread is connecting you to the greater body of belonging.

—Toko-pa Turner

On the day we say our goodbyes, the people who leave my painting and creative retreats look radically different than the ones who gathered on the first day. It's not something I expected when I first started teaching, but I find it fascinating. So often, when a new group comes together for the first time, the room feels thick with anxiousness, excitement, and anticipation. It makes sense; everyone just walked into a room full of strangers with large blank canvases looming on the walls. By the final day—shoulders dropped, seeing and listening intently to one another, emotions moving in waves across our open faces—we have become a group.

On our final day, I ask the participants to share any aha moments or key understandings from our time together. I used to assume that after all the painting we'd done, they'd share a technique, tip, or some kind of creative breakthrough. Sometimes they do, but more often they talk about something that seems to have nothing to do with paint: many say that the connections they made with each other are their biggest takeaway by far.

Having spent much of my life as a shy, socially awkward person when it came to larger groups, I have an immense amount of compassion for this particular set of feelings and emotions. I also understand how important it is for humans to feel safe in order to access deeper levels of personal transformation. It warms my heart to hear that my gatherings feel like a safe place to forge meaningful connections. I know how nourishing my own community is to me, so over the years I've incorporated more ways to nurture the bonds of community in my workshops.

For example, rather than breaking out our paints right away, we spend our first hours together arriving gently, soothing the edges of our collective nerves, and connecting with each other in real ways that ensure a feeling of belonging and ease. To do this, we begin by orienting to the space by slowly walking around the room at a quarter of the speed we're used to moving. We imagine roots growing out of the soles of our feet with each step, and we turn our focus inward to notice our breath, the feeling of the air on our skin, and the beating of our own heart. All this serves to remind us that we are, indeed, alive and in this room together. This is happening and we are here for it.

Next, I invite everyone to start seeing through the eyes of an artist by getting curious about the shapes, colors, textures, beauty, light, and shadow in the room. We move mindfully about, collecting information and inspiration. I share reminders that whatever eventually happens on the canvases in the room doesn't matter. For now, we're taking the time to notice, really notice, the world around us. We play with the idea of being in awe of our surroundings, and little by little, we arrive more fully.

I then invite everyone to start seeing each other.

With this prompt, I feel the room tightening for a moment. It's subtle, but it's there. What does it mean to really *see* another person, and how do we handle the implied corollary that we are going to *be seen*? It can induce strong feelings of vulnerability in people, so I remind everyone to start with what feels safe in their body. This might mean taking a deep breath, relaxing their shoulders, or possibly opening their palms in a gesture of receiving. For those who are ready, it might mean holding eye contact for a brief moment, or even brushing hands as they pass by another open, welcoming palm.

As we move around the room, I share a phrase I came up with in college that I could use in moments of awkwardness or disconnection in new groups of people. I repeat to myself, "This is my family. I belong here. This is my family. I belong here." I invite them to try it on if it feels right. Next, I remind everyone that of all the things we could be doing right now, everyone in this particular room is doing *this*. Each of our separate journeys has led to us sharing this time and space together. This feels like magnificent common ground.

Over the next couple of hours, we discover more we have in common as well as divergent details of our unique lived experiences. We share stories and intentions, move our bodies, meditate, and slowly step over the unseen threshold of this new beginning. By the time we gather again the following morning, we've already been through something intimate. The walls we build to keep each other out have started to crumble. Just like that, we're beginning to feel like trusted friends.

Only then do we break out the paints.

Creating in Togetherness

Contrary to the quintessential image of the artist toiling away alone in the studio, painting together in a room full of people (strangers, no less) provides an intimate, communal, and revealing experience. The same holds true for dancing, writing, praying, or traveling in a group. When we have witnesses to our personal journey, it can feel both invigorating and intimidating. Either way, it can bring a startling new level of aliveness when we share an experience with others that pushes us out of our comfort zone.

When groups of people move through meaningful life experiences together, a natural magnification and bonding occurs. Sometimes we choose this kind of experience, like when we sign up for a retreat or participate in a marathon. Other times, situations beyond our control force us into the depths of our humanity together. This was certainly the case in the aftermath of Hurricane Katrina, where destruction and despair gave way to the most incredible coming together of community that I have ever seen. Consider how much we tend to grow and learn when we're forced outside our comfort zone. It's no surprise that working to overcome challenges in a group accelerates both personal growth and intimate connection.

Imagine moving through the ups and downs of a creative process with a room full of people. You might feel exposed, but if the group can meet you wherever you are with loving-kindness and encouragement, the experience can invite you to the occasion. For this reason, I'm careful to construct a framework for feedback that centers each painter's own creative process. For this reason, we don't share negative critiques or vague compliments. I find these can muddy a painter's personal sense of what's working or not working. Responses to the work focus on process rather than product. For example, instead of saying, "I love (or don't love) this particular part of the painting," we can say, "I see a lot of dynamic movement in this painting."

There's nothing better than feeling loving support and connection from other people. It reminds us of what's possible when we allow ourselves to be vulnerable and held. It inspires us to offer each other the loving regard we all deserve. However, it can also highlight any areas where this kind of support is missing in other parts of our life. I often see this in my gatherings.

I remember one particular moment at the end of a retreat in Bali when I was swimming in the pool with a wonderful woman from Australia. She expressed her gratitude for the experience and all the connections she had made, but she also shared how anxious she felt about returning home to a place without this kind of soulful community to hold her.

After listening to her sincere desire for community, I asked her how she might use this longing as fuel to create what she truly wanted. Right there in the pool, we brainstormed ways she could foster a creative community by hanging posters in her local art shop, reaching out through online platforms, and hosting an art night in her studio.

A few years later, she showed up at another retreat bursting with excitement to tell me about the incredible group of women who now gathered every week in her hometown to create, commune, and support one another. This community had become the most meaningful part of her life.

The best part of that story to me is that she made it happen herself. Instead of waiting for someone to knock on her door to invite her to join the art community of her dreams, she became the inviter. She transformed what appeared to be a lack in her life into the exact inspiration she needed to manifest what her heart truly desired. Can you imagine how good it felt for the people who received her invitation? Even if they weren't able to say yes, simply being invited is a powerful act of inclusion.

After years of witnessing the magic that happens in my retreats when people are able to be vulnerable with one another, I now see this aspect of the gatherings as a vital creative act in itself. When we allow ourselves to connect deeply with another person or a group of people, we are essentially creating a new living relationship born out of the alchemy of what each of us brings to the table. Because of this, I always like to remind everyone in our opening circle that there is a reason we have come together and that each person brings an important and unique ingredient to the table that adds to the dynamic, complex flavor of the group.

For this reason, I feel that coming together with the intention to create, share, soften, and heal offers one of the most courageous creative and generative acts we can participate in.

Think of someone in your life with whom you share a deep connection. Imagine that you exist within one bubble and they exist within another. Now imagine that your lives coming together creates a third bubble—a separate entity that exists only because of the connection you share. In many ways, it serves as a dynamic intersection where two lived experiences inform and inspire one another in new ways. It expands your personal aliveness into a collective alive space.

Think of two primary colors, like blue and yellow. When they come together into the color green, they create something totally new and lovely—something that couldn't exist without both of them.

You might want to stay safe inside your own bubble or color scheme, and sometimes this is exactly what your nervous system might need. But I believe that this yearning for safety often masks a deeper craving for connection. Of course, often these connections are waiting just outside the edges of your comfort zone. At a retreat, for example, by sharing authentic transformational experiences with other people, you tap into a more communal and physical experience, which can allow you to access parts of your aliveness that otherwise might stay buried for a very long time.

Opening up like this can plop us down in vulnerable territory, but as Brené Brown reminds us, "Staying vulnerable is a risk we have to take if we want to experience connection."

Living a creative life means creating a life that works for you, and this often means coloring outside the lines of what is expected or what other people are doing. Blazing this kind of singular trail can be invigorating, but it can also be lonely. This is yet another reason to seek out and find kindred creatives who share in your desire to create life on your own terms.

Making Meaning with Others

"I want you to see me falling deeply in love."

"Please envision me feeling free of pain and full of vitality in my body."

"Help me imagine feeling fulfilled and grounded in a new career."

For years, I've been gathering multiple times a year with a group of women who all run creative businesses. We come together with the intention of supporting each other in whatever ways we can. These statements came out of a recent gathering, at which my friend Melody Ross asked each of us to share how we wanted to be held in the minds of the rest of the group in the coming year. Inspired by this thoughtful inquiry, we wrote out and shared snapshots of what we hoped the next year would hold. We took each other's desires into our care and decided to share in nurturing these visions for one another.

This and other profound connections, insights, and collaborations that surface from our time together never cease to amaze me. Coming together as individuals, we create a fertile soil for discovery and growth that is so much richer than any one of us could make on our own.

Melody also suggested that we each share a personal symbol as a reminder to the group to remember these requests. My symbol is a flock of Canadian geese. Every time I see one now, which is surprisingly often, I notice what's happening in that moment and remember all the ways I dreamt of becoming. When I see the shape of a pyramid, I think of another participant's deeply held wish and let my supportive energy flow in her direction.

With a little creativity, there are so many ways to infuse more meaning into how we come together and show up for our people. Over the years, these gatherings have not only brought much-needed clarity to my business, but they've also cultivated long-lasting friendships that are among my most cherished relationships.

I believe deep in my bones that one of the greatest gifts we have access to as human beings is our capacity to connect and grow with one another. I know how vulnerable it can feel to risk this kind of opening. We have to bare our souls to one another, hoping that others will accept us for who we are and value what we bring. This tenuous space once again asks us to dance between comfort and risk, knowing that true connection requires both.

I've been single for the past year, tossing around in the tumultuous waters of online dating. I can't tell you how much resilience it takes to keep putting your heart out there again and again, knowing full well that it's been hurt before and will likely be hurt again. Sometimes I want to give up, but the stubborn part of me that loves love and believes in the power of human connection keeps pushing me to show up. Of course I want to protect myself from future pain, but I'm just not willing to forgo love altogether in order to avoid getting hurt. There are days I'm ready to create a hard shell around my heart, but I understand that sooner or later that same shell will keep me sheltered from the very parts of myself that make me feel the most alive.

Joy, freedom, loss, and pain are all part of being alive. Whether it's with a child, a partner, a friend, a pet, or a relative, our ability to love and be loved offers one of the sweetest and most life-giving parts of the human experience. It's truly the heart in the art of aliveness. Besides, from what I can tell, we're more afraid of old pain than we are of new love. But what has been will never be again; the world renews itself, over and over. Our vital work is to glean the lessons from past hurts and transform this pain into seeds of hope for what we know can be possible again.

It is our work to keep believing in love. It is our work to keep loving.

Try This On

Call to mind the last time that a loving community, whether it was familial or chosen, provided the nutrient-rich soil needed for you to flourish in new ways. How did receiving that kind of support feel in your body? Did you resist joining the community, or did you allow yourself to open up within it? What did you have to let go of in order to accept their support? What opened up as a result of feeling accepted and connected?

In your journal, jot down brief responses to the following:

- How I felt before this experience in community

- How I behaved at the beginning

- What surprised me

- What actions, if any, I was inspired to take as a result of my experience in this community

Once you've spent some time thinking about a past experience of community, consider whether you're craving support in another area of your life now. How might you invite that in?

Coming together magnifies and supercharges our powers of creativity, discovery, and healing.

14

Embracing the Layers

*Grief is praise, because it is the
natural way love honors what it misses.*
—Martin Prechtel

"Stage four ovarian cancer."

My mother spoke these words to me in early April 2015. The moment I answered the phone, before I even heard her voice, I knew something was wrong. Sitting in my car alone in Manzanita, Oregon, I felt the steadiness of life as I'd known it slide out from under my feet. A few days later, I flew to Wisconsin to be with my mom. I didn't understand then that I was stepping into what would become the most heartbreaking rite of passage of my life.

Seven weeks after that moment in the car, the earth slid away again; my mom passed into the spirit realm. Both the shortest and the longest weeks of my life, they shook me to my very core. Like a surreal movie, I watched my mom's athletic body grow thin.

I watched her scream and writhe in resistance in the middle of the night, followed by days of softness and surrender. As if outside my own skin, I watched as we laughed and cried and slow danced our way across the hospital floor, making our way between bed and bath. I watched as her hair fell out and her appetite disappeared. I also watched her ask every nurse about their kids, leaning in and curious about every stranger's life, even as her own slipped away.

On April 29, 2015, I wrote:

> I've never before felt my heart in such a physical way, like the organ itself sitting so heavily inside my chest. Every day I'm with my mom, I can feel it breaking and opening, expanding and contracting, changing the very core of who I am and how I see the world. Life has never felt so precious and in focus, so heartbreaking and profound, all in the same breath.

Reading those words still brings me to tears, but they also remind me of the incredible capacity and strength of my human heart.

On Mother's Day 2015, I found myself barely holding it together as I worked with my brother-in-law, Jeremy Szopinski (a fellow artist), painting my mom's casket in our dear family friend's garage. In silence, we layered in deep shades of her favorite blue, images of flowers, and sweet prayers for a safe passage to the other side. This was one of her last wishes, to have her casket hand-painted "by the artists in the family." She also asked for simple daisies, upbeat show tunes, and the requirement to wear name tags at her funeral. She never got to see our painting, but I know she loved it. It was the most unique casket around, just like her.

On May 15, 2015, I wrote:

As the dawn broke, and the birds started to sing, and a sliver of moon still hung in the sky, my beloved mama slipped peacefully from this earthly realm, while my sis and I held her hand. Carol touched the lives and hearts of every person who was lucky enough to know her, and she leaves an extraordinary legacy of love, service, and community in her wake. I feel so honored to be her daughter and to carry her with me always. Rest in peace, sweet mama . . . may your spirit soar free.

When I lost my mom, I entered into a new room of the human experience—the room of grief. Yes, I had known sadness before, but this was altogether different. I'd certainly tried to imagine it, to prepare myself for its inevitability, but I've come to understand that the keys to this room only appear when the heart floods its banks. This place reaches beyond the emotional capacity of any previous rooms.

I could never have known when my mom called me that spring morning how many layers of experience I would embark on during and after her loss. It would be quite a while before I would be able to see any parallels between the process of grief and my creative life.

When I first entered the room of grief, it felt dark, heavy, and unfamiliar. I thought, *How could I possibly survive in this place, especially without my mom? In fact, how could I exist anywhere in the world without her?* Deep sadness, memories, and anger lurked around every corner. They pulled me into their stormy currents in the most unexpected moments. I would struggle up to the surface for air. Sometimes I had enough time to regroup and find my feet on the earth before the next wave hit, sometimes not.

I felt I could be stuck in that wild, crashing place forever.

A few months after my mom passed, I met an intuitive reader at a conference where we were both speaking. After a couple of days, she gently approached me to say she had a message for me from my mom, if I was interested. Of course I was curious, so we set up a time to talk.

She told me my mom wanted me to know how very special it was that we had overlapped on earth for forty whole years. She said our souls had been traveling together for many lifetimes and would continue to travel. Wasn't it wonderful that we got to experience being mother and daughter for this precious time?

Yes Mama, it was. I just hadn't thought about it quite like that.

The Revealing Humanity of Our Darkest Depths

Have you ever noticed that people who live through profound loss and rise up on the other side of it often possess deep-rooted wisdom and emotional depth? I think of them as trailblazers showing the rest of us that we, too, can survive hard things.

I'm drawn to people like this. I want to hear their stories and learn about the rooms they've been granted access to. I want to admire the hidden knowledge they've pulled from the darkness, so that I can understand my own journey. In return, I want to share the wisdom I've gathered in my own rooms of loss and grief. Whether through direct relationship, storytelling, song, or art, we can help each other through. Most importantly, I want to know their depth and run my fingertips along their scars. I want to remind them that their wounds are among their most beautiful and precious parts.

There is a richness in the mire and muck of our human experience. The more I learn to embrace the fullness of these muddy depths, the more I accept my own humanity. Over the last few years, I've nestled closer to grief, loss, and loneliness than ever before, and I've begun to understand the power of curiosity and gratitude in these moments.

Instead of pushing difficult emotions away, I'm learning to sit with and cultivate an interest in what they have to teach me. What if anger, grief, and fear were my mentors? Lately, in hard moments, I've been saying to myself, *Although it's painful, isn't it incredible that I get to experience these depths of human emotions—that I'm even able to be here for it?*

After all, this is what it feels like to be fully alive. What a gift it is to be here.

My mom didn't teach me about embracing difficult emotions while she was alive, just as her midwestern mom didn't do that for her. Yet, in her passing, I had the chance to unfold so many new layers of emotional understanding. Where I once would shy away from other people's grief, not knowing what to say and not wanting to offend, now I found that I could move toward others who were in pain. I could just be, holding them in immense compassion.

As I moved through those difficult first days and months, I felt called to attend a grief ritual led by the late Sobonfu Somé. I was desperate for tools to work with it. In a room of about eighty people, Sobonfu led us through the traditional ways in which her tribal community in Burkina Faso supported one another and processed their grief communally.

Together, we built three communal altars: one for our ancestors, one for forgiveness, and one for our grief. After the altars were built and candles were lit, we spent the next eight hours singing a simple chant that she translated for us as, "I cannot do it alone." We danced and drummed and sang. During this ritual, whenever a person approached the grief altar, someone from the group would automatically stand or sit behind them. As that person cried, yelled, and moved their anger and sadness through their bodies, this loving stranger would remain steady, holding space for as long as was needed.

The power of that support and the experience of grieving in community left me yearning for more traditions like this in my own culture. And yet any ritual holds the possibility of transformation. This is another way that artmaking and life braid together. Regardless of how you do it, painting has a number of rituals, from preparing space and canvas, to cleaning brushes, to the physical reality of time passing as paint dries. Each of these can be combined with the rituals described in this book, such as lighting candles or meditation, that enhance creativity and connection with spirit in artmaking.

I invite you to meet your grief, anger, or fear in a ritual space of your making. Rituals have a beginning, middle, and end. They might employ the elements of fire, air, water, and earth. They can be done solo or in community. Open your imagination to see the transformative rituals already around you. An end-of-summer bonfire, the marking of a birthday with a swim and candles on a cake, laying a memorial stone in the earth. Connecting in a profound way with these rituals allows us to transmute difficult feelings into gifts. Grief into compassion. Fear into insight. Anger into righteous hope.

Going Deeper Through the Creative Process

I spent the months that followed my mom's passing in my art studio, grateful to have a way to move my grief and anger out of my mind, through my body, and onto my big white canvases. Without this potent outlet, it felt like the sadness would've eaten me alive, or dissolved me into a never-ending sea. In difficult times, the creative process allows us to give shape to what we're going through outside our own bodies. It creates a safe distance to see ourselves, a way to digest and release what could become toxic if held inside. My painting sessions during that time took on even more ritual. I lit candles and carefully chose my music before scrawling big, drippy love letters to my mom as underlayers in my paintings. I welcomed the angelic forms that appeared and the way my fingernails could dig into the paint. I found solace in the many nights I spent crying and dancing and painting. Looking at those paintings now, I feel the incredible depth of the process I was in when I created them, but I also feel the soothing layer of time passed and the edges of heartbreak softened.

I also feel and see my mom in each of them.

Here's the thing. Paintings that go through the most challenging, ugly, or chaotic stages usually turn into the most interesting works in the end. When I embrace the ups and downs—either of emotional turmoil or a rocky artistic process—the resulting depth and beauty translates onto the canvas. When I block it or try to make it right, I cut off access to the layers that give the painting life. When I notice someone struggling emotionally in one of my workshops, their paintings tell the story. Visually, the painting conveys a sense of wild chaos. Or they may be fighting the urge to paint over everything, which would obliterate all their layers at once.

In these moments, I try to encourage the painter to lean into whatever is surfacing, because I believe that when we repress what's really going on, we get stuck. When we allow ourselves the space to be mad or sad or frustrated, or all of the above, we open up into movement and transformation. This leads us back to our aliveness, without fail.

In my many years as a retreat facilitator, I've watched the creative process evoke wild joy, deep sorrow, and everything in between. The unpredictable playground of artmaking stirs the pot but also provides a safe place to work with whatever comes to the surface in tangible, illuminating ways.

I remember watching one particular woman descend into sadness and anxiety during the middle of a workshop. Gently, I asked her what would happen if she allowed the feelings to come up and out onto her canvas. She decided that closing her eyes and painting with her hands might not feel too scary. She felt drawn to use yellow paint. To support her process, I switched up the music in the room to create a calmer atmosphere, and I'll never forget what happened next.

She closed her eyes and scooped up generous amounts of yellow paint. Poised with the paint in each hand in front of a dark, layered canvas, she just stood, breathing. I watched as her body began to sway to the music. Eventually, she reached out and touched the canvas with her fingers. Allowing the music to guide her, she began to move the yellow paint across the canvas with a slow and present sensitivity. Soon, I saw tears rolling down her cheeks. Eyes still closed, she continued to paint and weep and sway and release like this for the next few songs.

When she opened her eyes, she stared at her canvas for some time. I can still see her painting in my mind—light, wispy strokes of yellow danced across the chaotic layers beneath. The yellow marks radiated a pure, raw, honest energy. The contrast between the layers was powerful. When she'd finished, her face had softened and her shoulders dropped, as if she'd just released a very heavy burden.

Try This On

Major life events are like the layers of a painting. We can let go of how we think life is supposed to look and remember that each lived experience adds a new layer to our miraculous story. Loss, discontent, messiness, and the soul-stirring depths of the in-between can all combine into creating a stunning work of art. These raw materials also shape our resilience, depth, and character in the world.

Each layer and story of our life set the stage for the next chapter to unfold. It's tempting to want to bury the hard stuff in the past—but just as each layer in a painting informs the next, these very experiences have the power to show us the way forward.

This next exercise combines writing, movement, and drawing to explore how past life experiences connect to your present self and helps reveal how you can build the next layer of your journey.

Begin by remembering a challenging experience or chapter from your past. Notice how many years ago it happened and give yourself some time to write in a free-form way about the experience. For example, I might start my writing with, "Five years ago, I found out my mom had stage four ovarian cancer."

When you're finished writing, ask yourself what kind of body position might symbolize or bring to life what you wrote about. For example, I might put my hands on my heart and tip my head down. Find this position in your body, then move slowly between a neutral standing or sitting position and this symbolic position. Just notice how that feels. Stay in this physical space for as long as feels right, and then adjust so that you can draw a simple symbol in your journal that represents the experience. It might be interlocking hearts, an animal, or something more abstract. It could be anything.

Next, return to a neutral sitting or standing position and allow yourself to reflect on the present moment. What does your life look and feel like now? Start by writing, "Right here, right now . . ." and see where it takes you. Remember, there is no right or wrong way to do this. Simply allow whatever wants to surface to come through without overthinking it.

When you're done writing, repeat the physical part of the exercise by finding a new position in your body that reflects whatever you just wrote about. This might be looking up with arms stretched wide, palms to the sky. Now, slowly move between this position and your past position a few times, back and forth, noticing how this transition feels in your body.

Whenever you're ready, draw a symbol on your paper that represents the current you.

The final round of this exercise invites you to dream big into a future you'd love to create for yourself. I recommend looking forward to the same number of years that you looked back. For example, I would start my writing with, "In five years . . ."

Let your imagination run wild. Dream big. Think about where you will live, who you are surrounded with, and how you will feel in your body. What are you cooking, growing, creating, and wearing there? Have fun with the details of this glorious imagined future.

When you're done writing, move into a posture that represents your future self. For me, this might be standing, feet grounded, with a slight shimmy in my hips.

Now move slowly between your past, present, and future positions. Do this a few times, and notice how it feels to shift between these three parts of your life story. Do the movements evoke any emotion? Get curious about what's coming up for you.

When you're done, draw a symbol representing your future. If you'd like, play with how the three symbols you created might overlap to form one all-encompassing symbol. (Perhaps this is some fodder for a future tattoo or art piece?)

Remember, your story isn't over. While the chapters you've already lived are now in the past, you have the fortitude to decide how these foundational layers will support what unfolds next. Maybe your past experiences will be buried in paint, with only their textures adding to the complexity of the final piece. Or maybe bits and pieces of those early layers will remain visible on the surface, adding vitality, contrast, and depth. You get to decide.

Your life is your great work of art, every layer a part of your unfolding, exquisite story. There's no such thing as wasted paint.

Conclusion

Aliveness for a Broken World

I don't want life to imitate art. I want life to be art.
—Carrie Fisher

These are challenging times.

It can feel as if we're sinking into a swampy wasteland, thigh deep in rancid mud, thick weeds growing so high around us that they edge out the sky. I hear it in the exhausted voices of my loved ones. See it in the violent images and polarized vitriol of online spaces. Feel it in the clutching fear of environmental collapse.

And yet these are *our* muddy waters. We can't escape them or pretend they aren't there. So whenever I feel the swamp threatening to drag me down into apathy and despair, I take a deep breath. I remember: in art and in life, we work with what *is*. We choose our next layers. We feel the fear and do it anyway. We begin, and then we begin again.

Day after day, I find simple ways to infuse creativity into my daily routine, and I invite others to do the same. I walk in my neighborhood and feel the seasons shift on my skin. I sink my hands into the rich soil of my garden and watch growth turn to decay, offering nutrient gifts back to the soil. Looking at the state of the world, I dance and wail and paint it out.

I know of no better tool for an artist than presence. From presence, we discern reality. In presence, we speak the truth out loud, to ourselves and others. From presence we expand, decide to act, or wait patiently. Presence, of course, is one of the many facets of aliveness. Aliveness honors darkness and light, growing more palpable with the contrast. Aliveness renews our commitment to ourselves, our dreams, and the deep purpose we carry in our bellies.

Aliveness is creativity. Aliveness is movement. Aliveness is connection.

Like many of you, I often end up asking myself, *What do we need as humans to feel nourished, healed, inspired, and connected? What will it take for us to move past the polarization that comes from binary us-versus-them ways of thinking? How can we feel more alive and thus more compassionate?* I end up here because I believe nourishment, healing, inspiration, and connection lay the groundwork for wellness and creative thinking, which then lead to new solutions to global issues. In this way, what is personal is also planetary and vice versa.

Over the years, I've seen the ways in which color, music, movement, poetry, and creativity heal and awaken the human spirit. I agree with Carrie Fisher: I don't want life to imitate art. I want it to *be* art. I know it can be; I've experienced this firsthand. So many of us remain disconnected from the creative capacities in our own lives. Or we're dissuaded by old belief systems about what it means to be an artist. This leaves us feeling depleted, disconnected, and numb, covering up the burning desire so many of us have to create and feel connected to a kindred community through creativity. At the end of the day, we all want to feel inspired. We all want to belong. We all want to feel like capable creators in the world.

I believe we are living in a time of global metamorphosis, of colossal movement. This too is aliveness. With so much change comes an incredible amount of momentum for transformation of all kinds, from the personal and local to the global and universal. Within each contraction lies the possibility for new openings. With each crumbling, the chance to rebuild something fresh.

But what will it be? Here is where the aliveness of connection lays out our path.

With a change in perspective, the swamp in which we feel stuck reveals itself as something else entirely. From a bird's-eye view, it is a delta, a network of interlaced waterways and spits of land. A place where rivers mingle on their way to the sea. This delta is a liminal space that is neither river, lake, nor land. A vast community of plant and animal life makes its home here. I believe that the delta in which we find ourselves these days is similarly a transformational, fecund, connected, diverse, and alive place.

The Greek letter delta is also the symbol for difference. By spending time in this marsh, we learn to navigate the difference between solid ground and fluid waters. Between the layered past, the unfolding present, and the future we are all manifesting together.

Looking back, my own life seems to have meandered down so many disparate paths. And yet I see now how all the passions and rivers of my life have flowed into this delta, where they now merge and support one another. For example, I see how my years as a yoga instructor prepared me to teach my first painting class. How my love of dance, writing, and the natural world served to create a soulful painting experience that resonated with other creative seekers. How writing for myself as a means of exploring my inner world became a tool to branch out yet again in the pages of this book. I'm awed by the connecting streams of my life in their current creative flow.

I love to remember that mine is no solitary story, any more than a single tree standing in the forest lives on its own. Each tree enjoys the support of a vast, interconnected web of roots and mycelium in direct conversation with other plant life just beneath the forest floor. I too am gratefully intertwined with communities of many kinds, all over the world. These connections feed and nurture our mutual aliveness.

And new seedlings and rivers are always form-
ing. For example, after my years of singing lessons
with Leslie, I'm now learning to play the ukulele. This
foray into this tiny stringed instrument makes me feel
quite vulnerable at the moment because it's new, I'm
far from skilled, and I have a lifelong story running
through my head that I'm not musically inclined. Yet,
every single time I reflect on what my soul is craving,
it tells me loud and clear, *I want to play music and sing!*

When I reflect on this urge to make music, I see
how it's simply another form of creativity, one that's
been neglected for a very long time. As a creative person who values self-expression and as a woman who's
becoming more and more comfortable using my voice,
it makes sense that my desire to create music is surfacing now. I also appreciate how being a beginner in a
creative field will support my work as a more compassionate teacher. It's all connected.

Finally, aliveness as connection is teaching us all
how to tie our extraordinary gifts to their reciprocal
needs in the world. Now more than ever, we are living
in a time that requires each of us to show up in radical,
unique ways. No one way of thinking, being, or participating will turn the tides of these rough waters. The
complex challenges we face require each of us to reflect
on how our particular set of gifts, circumstances, and
privileges might serve the greater good.

Curiously examining this information while
simultaneously paying close attention to what makes

us feel the most alive has the power to unlock new paths forward while shedding light on what can otherwise feel like a pretty overwhelming situation.

So let's try on one more thing.

What about You?

What things have you been naturally drawn to over the course of your life? Let's focus on the things you enjoyed for you and not the things you did because others said you should. Can you identify themes or activities that have woven their way throughout your life from the beginning? Can you dive beneath the surface of these individual pursuits to find the roots that connect them all?

Next, write down the needs or pain points you see in your own life and your surroundings. What is crying out for help in your family, your neighborhood, and your community? What is breaking your heart and thus calling you into action? Notice if there are any obvious or subtle overlaps between these needs and the threads that create the fabric of your life and interests.

Another powerful way to gain clarity is to ask a few trusted people in your life to give you honest reflections about your gifts. Ask them, "What are the first three positive qualities that come to mind when you think of me? What do you depend on me for? What do you admire about me? What can you imagine me doing with these gifts that I'm not already doing?"

Asking for this kind of feedback might feel awkward at first, but receiving this information will likely be worth it. Sometimes we lose track of the things that come most naturally to us because they are just so, well, natural! Our trusted people see us in ways we can't or don't see ourselves, so lean into them. Ask for support and offer yours back in return. It's often this kind of honest conversation that serves as an opening to deeper connections and new insights. And who knows? Someone in your life might just have the exact observation you need to help you utilize your gifts for good for yourself and the world (just like Anahata did for me).

Remember, your baby steps can be things like taking a walk and opening up your senses or moving your body in a new way. Maybe you're ready to sign up for a class you've been eyeing or to reach out to a person you crave to meet or know more deeply. Maybe there are rivers in your life that feel ready to flow together to form something entirely new and utterly unique to you.

We all feel it, and sometimes it can seem as though we are too small in the face of life's enormous complexities to offer anything of value. But I can tell you, with utter confidence born out of so many beautiful, shattering, loving, and despairing experiences of my own, that every time you take even the smallest step toward living a life shot through with authentic aliveness, you are helping to create a world in which compassion, giving, creativity, and true community can survive—and thrive.

It's time to listen in, feel the fear, and do it anyway. All hands on deck, all rows in the water. As you move toward what inspires you, if it gets overwhelming, remember that you can always take a step back, recalibrate, and break your goals down into smaller, more doable micromovements. You can commit fully while staying open to change. You can strengthen your core and still work to soften your body and mind into greater responsiveness. You can dance between comfort and risk, passing the baton to others as you tap out to rest, and nurture the path of ease and joy as you go.

In these times of heartache and possibility, now more than ever, our aliveness asks us to acknowledge our own exquisite, messy tangle of life experiences and how they made us feel. These are the gifts we are meant to develop, cherish, and share with reckless abandon.

What a tender honor, to celebrate the art of aliveness with you.

Acknowledgments

I wrote this book during a global pandemic in my forty-fifth year around the sun, which I can only hope is my halfway point. The profound and ordinary experiences I've had thus far and the extraordinary people I've traveled through them with are really what wrote this book. I just tried to connect the dots and distill the gems.

In particular, I want to thank my mom for cheering me on so steadily in her first act and for breaking my heart so wide open in her second. To my dad for showing me what living completely in the present moment looks like at age ninety-four. And to my sister, Erin, for always being there, no matter what, from day one.

To Pixie Lighthorse and Melody Ross for the inspiration, clarity, and mad note-taking skills that grew the scattered seeds of these ideas into fully formed thoughts. To the rest of the Radiate crew for being the creative community of my dreams. To Rebekah Uccellini, Cvita Mamic, and Jonathan Wood for the infinite ways you teach me about the art of aliveness. To Lynzee Lynx for being my creative copilot and chosen family. To Emily McDowell and Shannon Sims for keeping me sane and laughing my ass off during quarantine. To Tina Grecchi for helping me make my wild ideas a reality and to Zippy Lomax for witnessing so much of it through your camera lens.

To Pearl Dog for being the best fur child and writing companion a gal could ask for.

To Randy Davila for believing in this book before I did, and to the editorial team at Hierophant Publishing for helping me bring it to life.

And to my global community of brave painters, who teach me endless lessons about life and art.

I am forever grateful.

About the Author

Flora Bowley lives and paints in Portland, Oregon. She is a permission giver, gentle guide, and the author of *Brave Intuitive Painting*, *Creative Revolution*, and *Fresh Paint*. She is also the illustrator of a children's book, *Earth is Holding You*. Flora reminds people that they, too, are artists, and she believes creativity in all its forms is what will save the world. She can often be found walking through mossy forests with her dog, Pearl, dancing while she paints, and dreaming of her next bold move.

Find out more at florabowley.com.

Hierophant publishing

books that inspire your body, mind, and spirit

Hierophant Publishing
8301 Broadway, Suite 219
San Antonio, TX 78209
888-800-4240

www.hierophantpublishing.com